MAXIM GORKY

Summerfolk

a new version by
Nick Dear

from a literal translation
by Vera Liber

ff

faber and faber

First published in 1999
by Faber and Faber Limited
3 Queen Square, London WC1N 3AU

Typeset by Country Setting, Kingsdown, Kent CT14 8ES
Printed in England by Mackays of Chatham plc, Chatham, Kent

A CIP record for this book
is available from the British Library

ISBN 0-571-20398-1

2 4 6 8 10 9 7 5 3 1

Summerfolk

Maxim Gorky (1868–1936): plays include *The Philistines* (1901), *The Lower Depths* (1902), *Summerfolk* (1904), *Children of the Sun* (1905), *Barbarians* (1906), *Enemies* (1906), *Vassa Shelesnova* (1910). One of the great Russian dramatists whose political grasp and rigorous examination of bourgeois values can be regarded as a complement to the Chekhovian canvas.

Nick Dear: theatre credits include *The Art of Success* at the RSC and at Manhattan Theatre Club, New York (winner of the John Whiting Award, 1986, and nominated for an Olivier Award), *Zenobia* (1995), *The Last Days of Don Juan* (after Tirso de Molina, RSC, 1990), *In the Ruins* (Royal Court, 1990) *Food of Love* (Almeida, 1988), *A Family Affair* (after Ostrovsky, Cheek by Jowl, 1988), *Temptation* (RSC, 1984). He has written the libretti for two operas, *A Family Affair* (1993) and *Siren Song* (1994), both premiered at the Almeida Opera Festival. His screenplay of Jane Austen's *Persuasion* was shown on BBC-TV in 1995.

Summerfolk in this version by Nick Dear was first performed in the Olivier auditorium of the Royal National Theatre, London, on 3 September 1999. The cast was as follows:

Sergei Bassov Roger Allam
Varvara Bassova (Varya) Jennifer Ehle
Kaleria Derbhle Crotty
Vlass Mikhailich Raymond Coulthard
Pyotr Suslov Oliver Cotton
Yulia Suslova Victoria Hamilton
Kirill Dudakov Simon Russell Beale
Olga Dudakova Beverley Klein
Yakov Shalimov Henry Goodman
Pavel Ryumin Jasper Britton
Maria Lvovna Patricia Hodge
Sonya Gabrielle Jourdan
Semyon Dvoetochie Michael Bryant
Nikolai Zamislov Jim Creighton
Maxim Zimin Jack James
Pustobaika David Weston
Kropilkin Liam McKenna
Sasha Elizabeth Renihan
Woman from the Kitchen Myra Sands
A Beggar Aislinn Sands
Complaining Actor Robert Burt
Young Actress Alex Kelly
Leading Man Martin Chamberlain
Semyonov Richard Henders
Mother in the Play Leigh McDonald
Servant in the Play Ceri Ann Gregory

Director Trevor Nunn with Fiona Buffini
Designer Christopher Oram
Lighting Designer Peter Mumford
Music Steven Edis
Sound Designer Paul Groothuis
Company Voice Work Patsy Rodenburg

Characters

Sergei Bassov, forty
Varvara Bassova, his wife, twenty-seven
Kaleria, Bassov's sister, twenty-nine
Vlass, Varvara's brother, twenty-five
Pyotr Suslov, forty-two
Yulia Suslova, his wife, thirty
Kirill Dudakov, forty
Olga Dudakova, his wife, thirty-five
Yakov Shalimov, forty
Pavel Ryumin, thirty-two
Maria Lvovna, thirty-seven
Sonya, her daughter, eighteen
Semyon Dvoetochie, Suslov's uncle, fifty-five
Nikolai Zamislov, Bassov's assistant, twenty-eight
Max Zimin, twenty-three
Pustobaika, fifty
Kropilkin
Sasha, Bassov's maid

The amateur actors
Lady in a Yellow Dress
Young Man in a Check Suit
Man in a Top Hat
Semyonov
Two Young Ladies
Cadet

Also
Servant Woman with a bandaged face
Beggars

Act One

Night. Outside the Bassovs' dacha.

To the rear, the terrace, with doors leading into Bassov's study and the house itself. At the front, an open area where people may sit outside. A piano stands under the trees. There is a table and wicker-style furniture.

Bassov can be seen through the open door to his study, working at his desk in the light of a reading lamp. Varvara enters quietly. She carries a book. She lights a match and holds it in front of her face. Bassov hears her strike the match.

Bassov Who's that?

Varvara Only me.

Pause. The match goes out.

Did you take the candle?

Bassov I did not.

Pause. Bassov doesn't move.

Varvara Ring for Sasha, please.

Bassov leans across to pull the cord of a bell near his desk. We hear it ring, distantly.

Bassov Useless house, this. Can't get a single draught of air through any of it. I'm sweltering. – Vlass here yet?

Varvara I don't know.

A silence.

Bassov Are you still there?

Varvara Yes.

Bassov Are you sweltering too?

Varvara Yes.

Bassov See what I mean?

Sasha enters from the house.

Varvara We need a light.

Sasha nods and turns to leave.

Bassov Sasha, is Vlass here yet?

Sasha Not yet, no.

Sasha leaves. Bassov hums to himself as he collects together his papers. Sasha returns with a lamp which she sets on a small table. Then she empties the ashtray into her pinafore. Varvara settles down in a chair by the lamp and opens her book.

Bassov He's become rather slack, your brother. Lazy. Always late. Recently he's been behaving very oddly.

Varvara Would you like some tea?

Bassov No, I'm just going to the Suslovs'.

Varvara Sasha? Run across to Mrs Dudakova, ask her if she'll come and have tea with me.

Sasha nods and exits into the house. Bassov locks his papers in his desk drawer.

Bassov Done . . .!

He comes out of the study, stretching.

Have a word with Vlass, will you, Varya? Tactfully, I mean?

Varvara Have a word about what?

Bassov About, you know, his duties. Tell him he should be more conscientious. Hmm?

Varvara Very well. I'll try. But I really don't think you should talk like that about him in front of Sasha.

Bassov Why ever not? The servants know everything anyway. – God, it's bare in there! (*indicating his study*) Can't you put something on the walls? A few of those nice frames with the funny coloured things inside – what do you call them? Paintings. (*He laughs at his joke.*) Right, I'm off. May I kiss your little paw?

> *Varvara holds up her hand, absently, still concentrating on her book. Bassov takes it in his hand.*

How chilly you are towards me. And how silent.

> *He bends to kiss her hand.*

And how bored you seem. Why is that?

Varvara Are you in a hurry?

Bassov Yes, I want to play chess with Suslov.

Varvara Then why don't we postpone our investigation of my mental state until you're not so busy?

Bassov Varya, there's no need to –

Varvara (*gently*) Well, it can't be that important, can it?

Bassov (*letting go of her hand*) I was merely making a comment, out of concern for your welfare. You are a wonderful woman, you know. If there was something annoying you . . . involving me . . . you'd say, wouldn't you? Of course you would. – You have a very odd look in your eye. Are you feeling unwell?

Varvara I'm perfectly fine.

Bassov You ought to find something to occupy your time with, my dear. You read too many books. You never stop reading! You can have too much of a good thing, if you see what I mean. One must try to curb one's excesses.

Varvara I hope you'll remember that at Suslov's. When you're on your third bottle of wine.

Bassov (*laughs*) Touché! But it's not the same case, not at all. These modish books can do far more harm than a few tots of Crimean red. Literature's a dangerous drug, particularly so as we know it to be manufactured by nutcases. Speaking of literature, Shalimov's descending on us any day now, isn't he? Wonder how he's turned out. Conceited, probably. Full of himself. Spend a few years in the public eye, you become unhealthily obsessed with your image. It's a well-known fact: writers are abnormal. Look at Kaleria – though whether we can legitimately call her a writer is a matter for debate. She's mad enough, mind. Maybe she should marry Shalimov . . .! Now there's a match! She's a bit on the old side, granted, a bit past her prime so to speak; also a dreadful whinger, as if she had permanent toothache; and let's face it, hardly a raving beauty . . .

Varvara Sergei, you talk the most awful drivel.

Bassov I do, don't I? But it doesn't matter. We're on our own.

Hidden in the trees, Suslov coughs.

Who's that?

Suslov (*emerging*) It's me.

Bassov (*greeting him*) I was just coming to see you!

Suslov Well, I'm just coming to fetch you! (*kissing Varvara's hand*) Have you been in town today?

Bassov No. Why?

Suslov (*with a wicked smile*) Your assistant. He won two thousand roubles at the club.

Bassov God, did he?

Suslov That's what they say. From a merchant who was paralytic drunk.

The men laugh.

Varvara Why must you always do that?

Suslov Do what?

Varvara Cut people down. Zamislov won some money. But only from a drunk . . .

Suslov (*grinning*) Me? Cut people down?

Bassov Oh, who cares. If he'd purposely made the chap drunk, and *then* won at cards . . . well, that might be below the belt, if you see what I mean. But it wasn't the case. Pyotr, shall we go?

Vlass enters from the house, carrying an old briefcase. He bows comically low to Bassov.

Vlass *Mon cher patron* . . . life must have been dull in my absence, I do apologise. Actually no I don't – you'll see what a difference my company makes. (*to Suslov, menacingly*) There's a character looking for you. He's creeping from one house to the next, asking where you live. Highly suspicious.

Suslov Hell's bells. I expect that's my uncle.

Vlass (*kissing Varvara's hand*) Hello, Varya.

Varvara smiles at him.

Bassov (*to Suslov*) Not a good time to visit, then?

Suslov Never been a better. I've no intention of being left alone with an uncle I've avoided for ten years.

Bassov Vlass – come into my study.

Bassov leads Vlass into the study, where he takes the papers from his desk. Suslov lights a cigarette.

Suslov Would you care to join us, Varvara?

Varvara No thank you. Your uncle, is he a poor man?

Suslov Why, you think it's only my poor relations I can't stand the sight of? No, he's stinking rich. – I say, keep an eye on that Zamislov. He's bent. We don't want him dragging your husband down into the mire, do we?

Varvara I've no wish to discuss such matters with you.

Suslov (*shrugs*) Don't say you weren't warned. – You do go in for direct dealing, don't you? Oh, you do enjoy a candid line of chat . . . Rather difficult to maintain, I should imagine, the bravura role of the straight talker. Requires a thick skin and a cast-iron character, not to mention fearlessness, integrity, et cetera, et cetera. Tell me if I'm being offensive.

Varvara You're not.

Suslov Aren't you going to argue with me?

Varvara No.

Suslov You agree with every word, then?

Varvara (*simply*) I don't know how to argue. Sometimes I don't know how to talk at all.

Suslov Fair enough. But you don't seem to understand how hard it is to live among people who insist on being truthful. It's hard.

Sasha enters from the house.

Sasha Mrs Dudakova's on her way, ma'am. Shall I make the tea?

Varvara Yes please.

Sasha And Mr Zamislov is here.

Sasha exits. Suslov puts his head around the study door.

Suslov Sergei, can we make a move?

Bassov Two seconds.

Zamislov enters from the house. He kneels to kiss Varvara's hand.

Zamislov How charming to see you, Madame. (*to Suslov*) Good evening, Suslov.

Suslov Good evening to you, you butterfly.

Zamislov Butterfly? (*He laughs.*) Why I admit, I am light as a feather. Light on my toes, and light in my pockets.

Suslov If you're referring to your strange mincing gait, I'll buy that. But as for your pockets . . .

Zamislov You don't 'buy' that?

Suslov They say you took some mug to the cleaners last night.

Zamislov The technical term is 'won at cards', Suslov, not 'took some mug to the cleaners', which implies an element of deception.

Varvara I am always hearing of your incredible exploits. You must be a very extraordinary person.

Zamislov When I hear the tales of my exploits, fair lady, I too become convinced of my uniqueness. Sad to say, I won only forty-two roubles.

Bassov enters.

Bassov Forty-two roubles? And I thought you were treating us to champagne. Well, sir? I'm in a hurry. Anything to report?

Zamislov Nothing that can't wait, if you are pressed for time. (*to Varvara*) Such a pity you weren't at the play, Madame! Yulia's performance was entrancing . . . luminous . . .

Varvara I always enjoy her acting.

Zamislov (*enthusiastically*) She has fantastic talent, I sincerely believe! I'd put my head on the block for it!

Suslov Be a shame if you were wrong, then, wouldn't it? Not very convenient, no head. – I say, can we get a move on, Sergei?

Bassov Directly.

Suslov Goodnight, Varvara. (*to Zamislov*) Goodnight, butterfly.

Bassov turns back to the study, where Vlass is sorting papers at the desk.

Bassov A fair copy by nine in the morning, I trust?

Vlass Do trust me, *patron*, oh do. (*aside*) And I hope you lie awake all night, fretting.

Bassov and Suslov exit through the trees.

Zamislov I must leave too.

Varvara Won't you stay for some tea?

Zamislov I would be honoured to return a little later. But not now . . . I must go . . . (*He quickly kisses Varvara's hand, and exits in a different direction.*)

Vlass Varya, why is there never any tea in this house?

Varvara Ring for Sasha. She's slow.

Vlass rings the bell in the study, and then comes outside. Varvara puts her hand on his shoulder.

You look exhausted.

Vlass I am. From ten until three I was in court. From three until seven I ran around town on office errands. From seven until now I was making my way here. From just then until a moment ago I was listening to you. It's all quite debilitating. Plus I missed lunch.

Varvara I wish you weren't a clerk, Vlass. It's beneath you.

Vlass Well, the great thing about doing a job that's beneath you is you don't have a chance to get above yourself, as the actress could conceivably have said to the bishop, depending on his –

Varvara Stop it, you idiot! Why must you be such a clown? Why can't you find work which has some meaning?

Vlass Madam! I must protest! Do you imply that the law of Imperial Russia is void of meaning? How dare you! I devote myself body and soul to a sacred institution, namely the defence of property and privilege against the incursions of the clamouring mass, and you deride me for a clown? Have you no moral fibre?

Varvara (*sighs*) Oh, be serious . . . just once in a while . . .

Sasha enters.

Vlass (*to Sasha*) Most respected and incorruptible lady, bring us a cup of tea.

Sasha Yes, sir.

Vlass And a bite to eat.

Sasha Right away, sir. How about a cutlet?

Vlass (*sings*) How about a cutlet? (*violently*) Exactly, a cutlet! Or anything with the essential qualities of a cutlet! Is it ready yet?

> *Sasha exits quickly. Vlass puts his arm around Varvara's waist and walks up and down with her.*

Something's the matter.

Varvara Vlassik, I feel very low. I don't know why. Suddenly . . . no particular moment . . . I seem to slump. I have no thoughts in my head, and then the walls close in around me, I'm imprisoned in . . . something. The world becomes strange and aggressive. The people in it frivolous and silly. And all you can do is play the fool.

Vlass (*strikes a comic pose*)
Pray don't think me a pain
For my gormless hilarity –
We're all trying to stay sane
In the face of reality.

. . . Rather better than Kaleria's efforts, I think we may agree. I won't go on to the end, we'd be here till – oh, come on, sister! What is this 'Be serious, Vlassik'? All the time, serious, serious! You're like someone who can't see, who wants everyone else's eyes put out!

Varvara That's enough! Stop talking! Just stop talking!

> *Sasha enters with food and implements, which she arranges on the table. Then she exits. In the distance, a watchman's whistle can be briefly heard.*

Vlass . . . Sure. And he fell silent. (*The briefest pause.*) But the thing is, you're not exactly being very sympathetic, Varya. I'm silent all day every day! Day in day out I'm silent! I sit there like a little mouse, making copies of slanders and duplicates of libels and generally biting my tongue – is it any wonder that at the end of the day I feel the need to crack the occasional *bon mot*?

Varvara I feel the need to go away. Somewhere. A place where simple people live, people sound in mind and body, where they speak honestly, straightforwardly, and do real, useful things! You know . . .?

Vlass (*thoughtfully*) Yes. I know. But you won't go, will you?

Varvara shrugs: 'Maybe.' Sasha enters with the samovar, which she sets on the table.

Varvara We're expecting Shalimov tomorrow.

Vlass Didn't like his last book. Wet.

Varvara I saw him give a reading once. When I was a student. I remember him up on the platform, full of strength and vigour, with his chaotic black hair . . . And his face, bold, honest, the face of a man who knows what he likes and knows what he hates . . . a man well aware of his strength. I watched from the hall and I tell you I was shaking, shaking with sheer joy, to think there were such people in the world! It was absolutely thrilling! And he'd toss back his hair with a vigorous hand, those thick locks like a lion's mane that hung around his shoulders, and his eyes would burn into you as if you were the only person present . . . Must be six years . . . no, seven . . . no, eight . . .

Vlass Are we indulging in a minor romantic fantasy? Watch out, sis – authors, as everyone knows, are slick and cold-blooded seducers.

Varvara That's not nice, Vlass. Don't be vulgar.

Vlass (*sincerely*) Will you please stop being angry with me?

They sit close together, hunched forward on their chairs, staring downwards.

Varvara Oh, I'm sorry. But try to understand. I'm waiting for him to come . . . like we wait for spring to come. I don't like the winter. I don't like my life.

Vlass I do understand, believe me. I don't like my life either. The act of breathing makes me feel ashamed. And who knows what the next instalment will bring?

Varvara Yes, that's it, that's it! Every episode worse than the last! But why must you –

Vlass Turn it all into a joke? I don't want them to see how wretched I am.

Kaleria enters from the trees.

Kaleria Above us, a vast bespangled canopy of night! And you two huddle together, your noses to the ground. Look up, I beseech you!

Vlass (*sighs*) Good evening, Kaleria.

Kaleria In the woods, no sound is heard . . . no sound but our thoughts . . . oh, glory! The honeyed moonlight, the silken shadows . . . Day can never be more beautiful than night.

Vlass Absolutely, couldn't agree more. Likewise girls can never be sprightlier than grandmothers, swallows can never fly faster than crabs, and –

Kaleria (*sitting*) You know nothing. Not a single thing. Varya, give me some tea. Has no-one been here?

Vlass No-one could be here or not here, for no-one does not exist nowhere.

Kaleria Begone. *Please.*

Vlass bows and goes into the study, where he begins sorting through the papers on the desk. Varvara pours tea. Through the trees we see the watchman (Pustobaika) pass, carrying a lantern.

Varvara Yulia Suslova came to see you.

Kaleria Yulia? Oh, about the play.

Varvara You went walking in the woods?

Kaleria I met Ryumin.

Varvara He's back?

Kaleria He talked about you. A lot.

Varvara What did he say?

Kaleria I think you can guess . . .

Pause. Vlass sings softly to himself.

Varvara It's very sad.

Kaleria For him or for you?

Varvara He once said it was a man's tragic duty. To love a woman. (*She says it with a little sneer.*)

Kaleria That's not the attitude you used to take.

Varvara Do you hold me responsible, Kaleria?

Kaleria No, Varya!

Varvara . . . I tried at first to soothe his melancholy. And I did, I admit, allow him a considerable amount of my time. But then I saw where it was heading. And then he disappeared.

Kaleria Did you ever confront him?

Varvara Oh, no! Not a word was said. Not directly.

Pause.

Kaleria Strange kind of love . . . lukewarm and weak . . . a lot of grand words, but no pleasure. For a woman, love without pleasure is an insult. Have you noticed he's a hunchback?

Varvara (*surprised*) Really? No! No, you're mistaken.

Kaleria There is a malformation in his soul. When I spot that, I can't help but see a physical defect as well.

Vlass comes gloomily out of the study, with a handful of papers.

Vlass In light of the multiplicity of suits and slanders allotted and after full and judicious consideration of this aforesaid fact, I request leave to approach you, learned madam, with a petition to the effect that, in despite of best endeavours, the chances of your humble servant copying out these depositions by 9 a.m. tomorrow are precisely nil.

Varvara I'll help you later. Have some tea.

Vlass What a sweet sister! Kaleria, learn a few lessons in friendship whilst there are still people like us to set an example!

Kaleria You are a hunchback, too.

Vlass From all viewpoints, or just side on?

Kaleria You have a stunted soul.

Vlass It's only in this jacket you notice it.

Kaleria Rudeness is a deformity. Like a hump. And stupidity is much like being lame.

Vlass And brunettes marry early. And most metaphysicians are deaf.

Kaleria That is not very witty.

Vlass Yes it is.

Kaleria Anyway, what do you know of metaphysics? Nothing!

Vlass Yes I do. It's like tobacco. I once tried smoking – I felt very sick and giddy. A dose of metaphysics produces similar effects.

Kaleria You've got a weak head. A bunch of daisies would knock you out.

Varvara Please try not to quarrel!

Vlass . . . I shall eat my cutlet. At least that serves some purpose.

Vlass turns away and concentrates on his food. Kaleria goes to the piano. She plays a few notes, then stops. Pause. Kaleria fans herself with some sheet music.

Kaleria It's so close tonight . . .

Varvara wanders towards the trees, looking up at the sky. A shrill blast on a watchman's whistle is heard. Varvara and Kaleria glance at each other. A moment later an answering whistle is heard. They seem to relax. Kaleria plays some more. Olga enters hurriedly from the house.

Olga Goodness, there are watchmen everywhere! Still, I'm here. (*She kisses Varvara.*) Dickens of a job getting away! Oh, Kaleria, dear, don't shake hands – play, play, I implore you! Hello there, Vlas!

Vlass Earth-mother, good evening.

Varvara Do sit down, Olga. Tea?

Olga Yes please.

There is another blast on a watchman's whistle.

Wait! – What's going on out there? It's put the jitters up me. As if something evil's lurking in the forest . . . Why do the watchmen blow their whistles like that?

Vlass To frighten us, I imagine.

Olga I would've been here sooner, but baby Nadya has the cholic, and Volka's feverish as you know. And Sonya insisted I bath her. And Misha got lost in the woods. And my husband returned from town in an atrocious mood, scowling like a beast. And as for the new Nanny . . .! She's driving me to distraction! Where the dickens do they find these girls? Boiled all the feeding bottles till they broke!

Varvara (*smiling*) Oh, you poor soul. You must be weary.

Vlass Too many hours in the kitchen, Martha. You've whipped yourself into a froth.

Kaleria What a puny metaphor.

Olga (*hurt*) I know you find me an object of mirth. I know how comical it must seem, me and my humdrum life. But what am I to do about it? We're all obsessed with our own misfortunes. In my case it's the children. Children! Whenever I hear the word, it's like a bell going off in my head! Children! If you'd any idea what a strain they are, Varya . . .!

Varvara Forgive me if I smiled. But it's not unknown for you to exaggerate a little.

Olga I don't see how you can say that. Who are you to judge? You haven't the faintest notion what a burden it is, raising a family. Being *responsible*. One day soon, they'll come to me and they'll ask: 'How should we live?' And what on earth shall I tell them?

Vlass Why tell them anything at all, in advance of having to? They might of course not bother asking. They might work it out for themselves.

Olga What do you know about it? They do bother asking – all the time! All sorts of scary questions, which no-one has answers to. Not me, not you, not anyone! It's so arduous, being a woman!

Vlass (*mutters*) You could always just try being human.

Varvara (*reproachfully*) Vlass . . .

Vlass goes quietly into the study, and settles down at the desk. Varvara again goes towards the woods.

Kaleria (*dreamily*) But dawn comes, finally, to kiss away the stars . . .

Kaleria leaves the piano and also goes towards the woods.

Olga Well. I seem to have depressed everybody. Oh, Lord. Well, I shan't bother coming any more. Don't you want me to visit any more, Varya? Is that why you've wandered off? Unless you come back I shall have to conclude you dislike me.

Varvara returns to Olga quickly.

Varvara Don't be ridiculous, Olga. It's just that I feel so . . . sorry for you.

Olga Don't say that. Don't. I know how repugnant I am. What an object of pity. My soul is all wizened, leathery, the skin of a very old dog. A horrid old dog that will bite you when you're not looking.

Kaleria The sun rises; the sun sets. But in our souls, eternal twilight.

Olga What are you talking about?

Kaleria Me? I'm talking to myself.

In the study, Vlass sings quietly, to the tune of a dirge-like Slavonic march:

Vlass
Family happiness
Family happiness . . .

Varvara Silence, Vlass!

Vlass . . . And he was silent.

Olga It's my fault. I goaded him.

Kaleria There are people coming out of the woods. Beautiful people! Walking out of a painting. Ryumin is waving his arms like an orator. (*Laughs.*) He's funny!

Varvara Who's with him?

Kaleria Maria Lvovna . . . Yulia Suslova . . . Sonya . . . Zimin, and Zamislov.

Olga (*wraps her shawl tightly around her*) And here's me looking like a drudge. That Yulia Fancypants – Lordy! She'll have a laugh at my expense. I don't like her one bit.

Varvara Vlass, would you ring for Sasha?

Vlass You interrupt the mute observance of my duties, Madame. Just for the record.

Olga She won't lift a finger for her children, that minx. What I find peculiar is, they never appear to be ill . . .

Maria Lvovna enters from the woods.

Maria Your husband said you're not feeling well. So what's the matter?

Varvara I'm feeling fine. Thank you for coming.

We hear chatter and laughter amongst the trees.

Maria There are worry-lines on your face. (*to Olga*) Oh, you've popped across, have you? Haven't seen you for ages.

Olga Probably because you don't want to.

Maria Why wouldn't I?

Olga Because I'm always in a sour mood.

Maria I may not like sweet things. Ever thought of that? How are your babies?

Yulia enters from the woods.

Yulia (*to Varvara*) I've brought a multitude! But don't panic, we'll be off again soon. – Ah, Olga. Hello. – Where are those boys? (*to Varvara*) Ryumin and Zamislov are with me. May they come in?

Varvara Why of course.

Yulia Come and help me round them up, Kaleria.

Yulia and Kaleria exit to the woods.

Maria (*to Vlass*) You've lost weight. Why?

Vlass Couldn't tell you. Lack of food?

Sasha enters from the house.

Sasha Will I make fresh tea?

Varvara (*nods*) Be quick.

Sasha exits with the samovar.

Maria (*to Vlass*) And why are you wearing that daft expression?

Olga He always does.

Vlass It's my speciality, daft.

Maria Very witty –

Vlass Thanks.

Maria – for a three-year-old. (*to Varvara*) Your Ryumin has finally hit the bottom. Mentally and physically.

Varvara What do you mean, 'my' Ryumin?

Olga Maria, I've been getting this frightful pain . . . and a cough . . .

Olga draws Maria aside and talks quietly to her. Yulia and Kaleria enter with Ryumin. Vlass takes one look at him and goes into the study, shutting the door behind him. A pause.

Ryumin Please forgive us arriving so late.

Varvara I love to have guests at any hour.

Yulia That's what's so gorgeous about the country. You can turn up anywhere whenever you like. Honestly, you should have heard them arguing! Him and Maria Lvovna!

Ryumin There are certain things one cannot remain equable about.

Yulia But nobody listens to you when you screech like that.

Sasha enters with the samovar, which she sets on the table. Varvara busies herself with the tea-service. Ryumin watches her closely. Sasha takes tea to everyone.

(*to Varvara*) Your husband's ensconced with my own ball and chain, halfway through a bottle of brandy. They'll end up drunk. Added to which my husband's uncle's turned up on the doorstep – he's in beef, or possibly bacon, owns a slaughterhouse at any rate, laughs like a drain, eats non-stop . . . ever so droll. But where's my Romeo? Wherefore art thou, Romeo?

Zamislov (*off, in the woods*) In the olive grove, fair maid.

Yulia Come here at once.

Zamislov enters from the woods.

What are you doing?

Zamislov Corrupting the young.

Yulia Oh, goody. How?

Zamislov Sonya and Zimin have been trying to tell me what life is for. They believe us to have been put here to spend our days solving moral and political problems. I have conclusively proved to them, however, that life is art – the art of seeing with your own two eyes and hearing with your own two ears.

Yulia What rot.

Zamislov Well, all right, I thought it up on the spur of the moment. I do believe, though, that I shall grow attached to my theory. For what is life, but the art of finding beauty and happiness in everything you do? – They're fighting like dervishes out there.

Yulia Can't someone get them to stop?

We hear Sonya and Zimin arguing in the woods. Sasha exits. Zamislov descends on Kaleria like a bird of prey.

Zamislov Kaleria, you love everything beautiful. Why don't you love me? It is too paradoxical for words.

Kaleria (*smiles*) You're rather flashy for my taste.

Zamislov Really? Lucky I wasn't serious, then, eh? In point of fact, what we desire – the fair maid Juliet and I –

Yulia Oh, shush, you're so embarrassing! (*She giggles. To Kaleria*) We want to beg a favour. May we go to your pristine little room?

Zamislov (*conspiratorially*) Too many members of the general public round here.

Kaleria (*amused*) Then we'd better go . . .

They start to go into the house together. Then Yulia turns back to the others:

Yulia Wait till you see my husband's uncle! I think he's escaped from the circus!

Zamislov laughs with her, and they exit with Kaleria.

Olga Well. Who would think, given her flighty manner, that life at their dacha is less than rosy? But apparently –

Varvara (*snaps*) That is none of our business, Olga.

Olga What have I said now?

Ryumin (*sighs*) Sometimes one feels one is living in a long-running matrimonial drama.

Sonya skips in from the woods.

Sonya Mama! We're going for a walk!

Maria Another walk?

Sonya Yes, another walk! This party's full of women, and you know how dull I find them.

Maria (*with a smile*) Tread carefully. It's been rumoured your mother's a woman.

Sonya Mama! You? No! Since when?

Olga What disrespect!

Varvara Yes, I don't think it would kill her to say hello.

Maria See, Sonya? Your bad manners don't go unnoticed.

Sonya (*to Varvara*) We've met twice today already! But I'll give you another kiss – making three – with the greatest pleasure. I can be very generous like that. It may be old-fashioned, but it is at least cheap.

Maria Sonya! Leave! You're too rude!

Sonya As for my mother, though, suddenly announcing she's a woman . . .! Eighteen years she's kept me in the dark! And now this bombshell!

Zimin pokes his head around from behind a tree.

Zimin Are we going for a walk or not?

Sonya May I introduce my slave, Mr Zimin?

Varvara Why don't you join us, Mr Zimin?

Sonya Oh, I won't bring him into polite company, Varvara. He is only a slave.

Zimin Excuse me, ma'am, but she's practically ripped the sleeve off my jacket, trying to get me to agree with her! Which I don't!

Sonya See? He likes punishment.

Zimin I'll stay here if you don't object.

Sonya He's insufferable. I better take him off for further tedious protestations of unyielding love.

Zimin Eh? I thought we were discussing class solidarity!

Sonya We were, but the moon just came out.

She gives him a shove out into the woods.

Zimin Don't push me, Sonya.

Sonya If you can be pushed, I'll push you.

Sonya, laughing, turns back to the others.

Goodnight!

Sonya and Zimin exit. They can be heard talking and laughing for some time.

Ryumin She certainly has some spirit, Maria.

Olga I was like that once.

Everyone looks at Olga with suspicion.

Varvara (*to Maria*) And you get on so well with her.

Maria We're friends.

Olga Friends? How on earth can you be friends?

Maria I'm sorry?

Olga She's your daughter!

Maria But it's terribly easy, Olga. You just have to be honest. Never deceive them. Never hide the truth from them.

Ryumin (*with a harsh laugh*) That's one hell of a risk! Never hiding the truth! The truth is hard and cold, and a great incitement to scepticism. Show a child the dreadful face of truth and you will poison their sensibilities at once.

Maria You prefer to poison them slowly? Lie by lie? So you can't even see yourself how you are ruining their personality?

Ryumin (*hotly*) Steady on! I did not suggest that at all! But I stand opposed to these foolish attempts to rip away the poetry with which we adorn life's saggy old body. Life must be dressed in miracles. It is an ugly thing. Prepare a new suit of wonders, before you strip it bare.

Maria I confess I have no idea what you mean.

Ryumin I mean we have a right to be deceived! About the nature of human existence! Because if you stare life straight in the face, what do you see? Some inscrutable beast which devours us, and sucks our blood, and mashes our brains just for pleasure! What the devil is it for? And the older you get, the more you become aware of the filth, the banality, the mediocrity, the injustice that surrounds us . . . and the more you crave purity and light . . . We can't escape the contradictions, and we haven't the strength, have we, to purge ourselves of the evil – so for God's sake allow us our right not to see the naked truth! Allow us to indulge the masquerade! All we want is to rest, peacefully, to be allowed to – to forget –

He catches Varvara staring intently at him, and comes juddering to a halt.

Maria Have we come to a climax? That was quick.

Ryumin (*to Varvara*) I'm so sorry.

Maria And now we want to rest. Hmm . . .

Ryumin I lost control again. Bellowing and –

Varvara Yes.

Ryumin You're angry with me.

Varvara Yes, but not for the reasons you think.

Ryumin Then why?

Varvara . . . Because you said something altogether different, two summers ago. Quite, quite different . . . but equally heartfelt . . . equally loud.

Ryumin Well, everyone changes their ideas, you know.

Maria Wicked little things, ideas, flitting through our heads like bats . . .

Ryumin Do you doubt my sincerity, Maria Lvovna?

Maria No, I don't. You're hysterical enough to be sincere, if not exactly persuasive. It is clear to me that you're a scared man, Pavel. You'd like to hide your head in the sand. You're not alone in that. Many people are frightened of life.

Ryumin That's true. And you know why? Because they can see how vile it is! They feel it more keenly every day! The whole business of existence is strictly predetermined, with one factor only being random and meaningless – human life itself!

Maria Try and reconcile the accident of your creation with the urgent need to reform society. You might find it takes on some meaning.

Olga Lord! Whenever I hear a heated conversation, I assume I've done something wrong! Time for me to go home, before I disappear into the depths of my own pointlessness. How I wish everyone could be nicer!

Varvara Stay, Olga.

Olga It's always very stimulating here, Varya. The vital parts of my intellect are always suitably tickled. But it's late and they probably need me.

Varvara If they need you, they'll send for you. Stay with us, please.

Olga I suppose they will send someone . . . if I'm needed . . . Well, I'll stay a few minutes. (*A pause.*)

Varvara Strange way to live . . . talking, talking . . . not much else. Full of opinions, aren't we? – learnt fast, thrown out even faster. But desire . . . the clear, fresh water of desire . . . do we have any of that?

Ryumin Are you referring to me?

Varvara I'm referring to us all. We lead ugly lives. Ugly and boring.

Yulia enters from the house, followed by Kaleria.

Yulia Ladies and gentlemen, I need your assistance!

Kaleria Must you?

Yulia Kaleria has a new composition, which she's agreed to recite at our Charity Night for the Orphanage – but I want to hear it now! Ladies and gentlemen, persuade her, please!

Ryumin Recite it for us, will you? I love your pretty verses.

Maria So do I. Too much argument leaves a bad taste. Please, let us hear it.

Varvara It's new?

Kaleria Yes, but it's dull. It's only a bit of prose.

Yulia Then you won't lose anything by reading it out, will you? If it's not really a poem?

Kaleria I'll need my music.

Yulia Well, let's fetch it! Come!

Yulia takes Kaleria by the hand and leads her back into the house.

Maria What happened to your brother?

Varvara Locked himself in the study. Awful lot of work.

Maria I was too hard on him. I get cross watching him act the joker all the time.

Varvara Isn't it tiresome? But if you could try being a little less aggressive . . . I think you'll find he's a decent man. Never been shown any affection, that's all.

Maria (*smiling*) Of course. Anyone would be the same.

Varvara He was brought up by father, who was a drunk, and used to beat him.

27

Maria I'll just go and say hello.

Maria goes to the study door, knocks and enters. She closes the door behind her.

Ryumin (*to Varvara*) You've become very close to Maria Lvovna . . .

Varvara I warm to her.

Olga Ooh, she's severe, though.

Ryumin She has the cruelty of the true evangelist. Blind, numb cruelty. How can you warm to that?

Dudakov enters from the woods, nervously.

Dudakov Ah, hello. Ah, yes – good evening everyone. Isn't it hot? – There you are, Olga. Coming home now?

Olga Yes. Immediately. Had a nice walk?

Varvara Will you take a glass of tea, Kirill?

Dudakov Tea? Ah, no thanks – never drink it in the evening. Pavel, I need a word with you. May I call tomorrow?

Ryumin Please do.

Dudakov Fact is, it concerns the Juvenile House of Correction. Yes, further trouble! The damned warders have been beating the damned children, according to yesterday's paper. And you and I are being held responsible.

Ryumin I haven't been out there for a good while, to tell the truth. Never seem able to find the time.

Dudakov Well, that's a familiar tale. No-one seems able to find the time. We're all busy being busy, but does anything ever get done? What is wrong with us? Myself, I get terribly tired . . . so tired . . . A little wander in the woods, that soothes the nerves, but generally . . . I'm feeling the strain.

Varvara You do look tense.

Dudakov Wouldn't surprise me. And today brings further tribulations. That, ah, buffoon of a Mayor has queried the accounts at the hospital! Apparently we're feeding the patients far too much, and prescribing too much quinine. Cretin! For one thing, it's none of his business; for another, if he'd improve the drainage at the lower end of town, the demand for quinine would dry up! What does he think I'm doing, drinking the stuff myself? I can't abide damned quinine! Nor can I abide busybodies!

Olga Kirill, you mustn't let yourself get in such a state over trivialities. You should be used to it by now.

Dudakov But my life seems composed entirely of trivialities! And what am I supposed to be used to? People sticking their nose into everything I do? Morons over-complicating my affairs? Ah, well, yes, put it like that, I'm used to it, sure enough! Make economies, says the Mayor! So be it, I'll make economies. The sick will suffer, but a healthy audit naturally takes priority. I'm not one of these Maria Lvovnas with a private practice, so I'm stuck in that stupid job –

Olga – because you've such a large family? Oh, I've heard it all before, Kirill, umpteen times! I don't know why you feel the need to dredge it up in public! Oh, you are a tactless man! (*She runs tearfully into the house.*)

Varvara Olga –

Olga (*off, sobbing*) Leave me be! I know what he says! I've heard him!

Varvara follows Olga.

29

Dudakov (*dismayed*) Damn. Did it again. I never mean to! My apologies, Pavel . . .

Dudakov exits quickly into the house, almost colliding in the doorway with Kaleria, Yulia and Zamislov, who are coming out.

Yulia What's the matter with him?

Ryumin Nerves are shot to hell.

Varvara enters from the house.

Has she gone home?

Varvara Yes. He's running after her.

Yulia I don't trust Dudakov. For a doctor, he's not exactly in the peak of condition. He sweats, he scratches . . . he stirs his tea with that little hammer he keeps in his medical bag! You won't catch me taking one of his prescriptions!

Ryumin I believe he'll put a bullet in his head, some day.

Varvara How can you say that so calmly?

Ryumin Doctors frequently commit suicide.

Varvara And words do more damage than people – don't you think?

Ryumin (*shudders*) Oh, now, Varvara . . .

Kaleria sits at the piano. Zamislov stands by her. The others gather chairs around to listen.

Zamislov Comfortable?

Kaleria Thank you.

Zamislov My Lords, Ladies and Gentlemen . . . your concentration please!

Enter Maria and Vlass from the study, both very animated.

Vlass So, we're going to have poetry? What larks!

Kaleria You'll have to be quiet if you want me to perform.

Vlass (*freezes*) The life-force froze within him . . .

Maria pulls Vlass into the seat next to her.

Maria We'll be good as gold!

Kaleria So glad to hear it. What I am to recite is a prose-poem set to music, of my own composition, which will in due course be orchestrated for string quintet.

Yulia A prose-poem set to music! How novel! I'm sure I'm going to love it. I love anything original, I love picture postcards, I love automobiles –

Vlass – I love earthquakes, I love tuberculosis –

Kaleria (*stroppily*) May I commence?

Maria tugs on Vlass's sleeve and he is silent. They all take their seats. Kaleria ripples through a few minor arpeggios.

It is entitled 'The Edelweiss'.

The peaks of the Alps. Enclapped in ice. Shrouded
   in snow. For all eternity.
And above them
Silence.
The kingdom of silence.
The wisdom of uncharted altitudes.

Beyond the mountaintops
The wilderness of heaven.
The sad, uncountable eyes
Of the stars.

Below
On the plain

In the province of Man, on the close-packed plain –
Life stirs.
Fearfully and fitfully
Man suffers and strives.

From the dark pits of the earth comes
Dissonance!
Cacophony!
Grim threnodies of life.
Cries of anger,
Cries of laughter,
Cries of love.

But the Alpine peaks
And the supine stars
Are unmoved.

Yet
Clinging to the ice-caps
Encased in awesome silence
Bearing witness to the torment of Man –
A perfect flower grows
Solitary and sad . . .
The Edelweiss.

She ends with a dying fall. Everyone remains deep in thought. Kaleria stares into space. In the distance, we hear a watchman's whistle.

Yulia (*softly*) Very fine . . . pure and fine . . .

Zamislov I know! You should wear a costume! White and diaphonous, like the Edelweiss itself! Wouldn't that be fiercely beautiful?

Vlass (*approaching the piano*) Even I liked it. It was jolly good! (*He gives an embarrassed laugh.*) So refreshing – like a cranberry juice on a scorching day!

Kaleria Go away.

Vlass I'm serious, Kaleria – I enjoyed it!

Sasha enters.

Sasha Mr Shalimov is here.

Ryumin The writer?

There is general commotion. Varvara approaches the door, but stops still as Shalimov enters from the house. His hair is cropped close to his head, and is completely grey.

Shalimov Have I the pleasure to –?

Varvara is staring at him in disbelief. Then she recovers herself.

Varvara Please, do come in. Sergei will be back shortly.

End of Act One.

Act Two

Sunset in front of the Bassov's dacha. A clearing surrounded by a dense ring of fir trees. There are pathways through the woods. Way back, to one side, is a small open-air stage, with benches before it. Various chairs and tables.

Pustobaika, a watchman, is mending a chair, as slowly as he can. Off-stage, a whistle blows. Pustobaika puts his own whistle to his mouth, and answers it. A moment later Kropilkin enters, a rifle slung over his shoulder, his whistle hanging round his neck.

Kropilkin All right?

Pustobaika All right?

Kropilkin (*indicating the direction from which he has come*) Who's got that one this year?

Pustobaika Suslov. Engineer.

Kropilkin New people, is it?

Pustobaika What you mean, new people?

Kropilkin Not the old people, as had it last year.

Kropilkin lights a cigarette. Pustobaika takes out his pipe. Clearly it's time for a break.

Pustobaika (*shrugs*) New people. Old people. All the fucking same.

Kropilkin Townies.

Pustobaika Yep. Summer folk. Fifteen years I been watchman here. Seen 'em all – lost count. They come and go like pimples on your arse.

Kropilkin (*laughing*) Pimples, right.

Through the woods pass a group of young people with balalaikas and mandolins. They talk and laugh, and exit.

Kropilkin Sounds like we're going to have some music!

Pustobaika (*sourly*) Marvellous.

Kropilkin (*indicating the stage*) And they're putting on a play, by the look of it.

Pustobaika Oh, they do that regular. Plenty of leisure time, you understand.

Kropilkin I never seen a play.

Pustobaika You ain't missed much.

Kropilkin You seen one, have you?

Pustobaika My boy, I seen dozens, and they're all the fucking same.

Kropilkin What they like then?

Pustobaika Nothing complicated about it. First, you dress up in clothes that ain't yours. Don't ask why. Next, you mouth off a lot of words, whatever takes your fancy sort of thing. You might be happy, you might be sad: don't matter. You possibly runs up and down a bit – but only on the platform, mind, you don't get off, that's forbidden.

Kropilkin Why?

Pustobaika Dunno. It is a bit restrictive. Then you all has a go at each other. Bit of fighting, bit of kissing if you're lucky – just do the first thing as comes into your head, far as I can see.

Kropilkin And that's it?

*Off, a man whistles for his dog, and shouts: 'Bayan!
Here boy! Come here! Bayan!' Off, to the other side,
we hear a throaty laugh from Dvoetochie.*

Pustobaika Yep. That's acting.

Kropilkin Well bugger me. I thought it was –

Pustobaika Well it ain't.

Kropilkin They sing a song or two, though?

Pustobaika Not as often as you might expect. The
engineer's wife has a go. Sounds like a goose with a
belly-ache.

Kropilkin (*putting out his cigarette*) Here they come.

Pustobaika (*picking up his tools*) Fine by me.

*Dvoetochie enters with Suslov. Pustobaika resumes his
work. Kropilkin marches off behind the stage with a
purposeful expression.*

Dvoetochie So these Germans turned up. Pots of capital.
My little outfit was old, the equipment obsolete. They
had the latest gear, could get through five times the
volume. Kept their prices low, see, began to undercut me.
I thought, you're on a hiding to nothing, my son. You'll
never beat a German. So I sold 'em the lot.

They sit down.

Suslov You sold the factory?

Dvoetochie I kept the house in town. Dirty great place.
Everything else, I got shot of. And now I've nothing
left to do but count my money. (*Laughs.*) Feel a right
bloody fool, to be honest. Sold up; felt like an orphan.
Nothing to do! Bored stiff! See these hands? Never
noticed them before. Now I keep finding them dangling
around, useless lumps of meat on the end of my arms . . .
(*Laughs.*)

Varvara comes out on to her terrace, and walks up and down, sunk in thought.

Bassov's wife, isn't it? Now that's what I call a woman. If I was ten years younger . . .

Suslov But I say, I thought you were, um, married, Uncle?

Dvoetochie Was married. And not just the once. They either died or ran away. Didn't stick around, whatever way you slice it. Had kiddies too . . . couple of little girls . . . they died. And a boy. He drowned. Ah well . . . But as far as women go, I have a certain expertise. Your Russian woman can't resist a stud like me! Piece of cake to take her off you! Know why? On account of you're pathetic bloody husbands! (*Roars with laughter.*) I'd roll in from Siberia, wiping the ice off my nose, spot some pretty filly – usually married to a toff in a daft hat – and fifteen minutes later I'd be holding her in my arms!

Vlass comes out on to the terrace, and watches his sister.

Yep! Easy as that! Then they either died or ran off. Ah well . . . (*Pause.*) Nobody left now.

Suslov So what are you planning to do?

Dvoetochie Not a clue.

Vlass What is it, Varya?

Varvara Nothing, I'm . . . I'm just being silly.

Vlass (*puts his arm around her waist*) I wish I could think of the right thing to say.

Varvara (*gently*) I'd rather you left me alone.

Hurt, Vlass leaves her and approaches Suslov and Dvoetochie.

Dvoetochie The boy Vlass is coming over.

Suslov Him? He's a laughing-stock.

Dvoetochie Got a lively enough mind . . . but lazy.

Vlass Who's lazy?

Dvoetochie My nephew here! (*He claps Suslov on the back and laughs.*) And you're not exactly a model of efficiency, are you, my lad?

Vlass I've not had the pleasure of your acquaintance for very long, Mr Dvoetochie, but as far as I can gather, your notion of 'efficiency' involves sucking the blood from your fellow man, is that right? In which case, no, I'm not a model of efficiency. Alas.

Dvoetochie (*laughs*) Don't lose any sleep over it! It's tough when you're young. Your heart hasn't hardened yet, and your brain, which should be steel, is pink blancmange. Give it a few years, you'll mature, and then riding around on your neighbour's back is – you'll find – the only way to travel.

Vlass I'm sure you've undertaken many lengthy journeys in that fashion.

> *Vlass bows cordially and exits.*

Dvoetochie (*laughs*) Look at him, like the cat who got the cream! Thinks he's given me a right walloping!

Suslov He's a layabout.

Dvoetochie He's all right; let him be a hero for a couple more years. Ah well . . .

> *Dvoetochie sinks into thoughtful silence. Kaleria comes out on to the terrace.*

Kaleria You still can't get used to it, can you?

Varvara No, I can't.

Kaleria Didn't it occur to you he might have changed? (*Pause.*) So who will you wait for now?

Varvara I don't know.

Kaleria shrugs, comes down from the terrace, and walks off behind the dacha. Dvoetochie suddenly seems to wake up.

Dvoetochie So, Pyotr! How am I going to live?

Suslov I don't think I can offer an immediate answer on that one, Uncle.

Dvoetochie What have you got against immediate answers?

Suslov I shall give it my earnest consideration.

Dvoetochie (*sighs*) I feared as much.

Bassov and Shalimov enter through the woods, and sit nearby. Bassov has a towel round his neck. Dvoetochie hails them.

Been for a stroll?

Bassov Been for a swim.

Dvoetochie Cold?

Bassov Bearable.

Dvoetochie I wouldn't say no to a swim. Come along, Pyotr!

Suslov Ah, no, I'm sorry, I can't.

Dvoetochie But maybe I'll drown, and you'll get hold of my money even sooner?

Suslov I need to talk to these gentlemen.

Dvoetochie Have it your way. You might have come into a fortune . . .

Dvoetochie exits. Suslov goes across to Bassov, shaking his head in mock despair.

Bassov Varya! Mr Suslov's in need of a drink. Send out a bottle of beer!

Shalimov coughs.

Bassov Better make that three bottles!

Varvara goes indoors. Suslov sits with the men.

Bassov How is the old boy?

Suslov Hellish.

Bassov They're not much fun at that age, are they?

Suslov I think he wants to come and live with me.

Bassov Live with you . . .? Could you cope with it, Pyotr?

Suslov God knows! I imagine he'll get what he wants.

Sasha enters and serves beer.

Bassov You've gone very quiet, Yakov.

Shalimov Feel like I've had the stuffing knocked out of me. What was the name of that warlike woman?

Bassov Maria Lvovna.

Suslov I say, you haven't been arguing with *her* . . .?

Bassov (*laughing*) All the way through lunch!

Shalimov She's one ferocious female, I tell you . . .

Sasha exits. Varvara comes back out on to the terrace.

Suslov I can't stand her.

Shalimov I'm a mild-mannered chap, but I nearly lost my self-control. I don't like to be rude.

Bassov She's got no such scruples!

Shalimov Look at it from my point of view: a chap sits down to write something, it's a devil of a job, you sweat blood over it, and when you're done, frankly, you're knackered. So your friend's got a dacha in the country. So you come down to rest and relax. Suddenly a fiendish woman appears out of the blue. And before you know it, you're on trial for your life. What do you believe in? What do you aspire to? Why do you write about this? Why are you silent about that? And more: you weren't clear about this, you lied about that, that's not convincing, that's not beautiful. Jesus! And you think to yourself: please, have a go, madam, see if you can write something that's sublime and convincing and true! I'm sure you're an undiscovered genius! Just leave me be!

Bassov Par for the course, my friend. If you row down the Volga, you eat sturgeon stew. If you meet an author, you suddenly become an intellectual. See what I mean?

Shalimov She's not an intellectual! She's a witch! Does she often stay down here?

Bassov God, no . . . well, a fair amount . . . But she's not one of my close friends. Too inflexible, no give and take. It's my wife who invites her round. She's a rotten influence, if you want my considered opinion.

Bassov looks round and sees Varvara, who is listening. He swallows hard.

Bassov Ah, Varya. Didn't know you were there . . .

Varvara (*coldy*) Didn't you.

Zamislov and Yulia come along the path from the direction of the Suslov dacha. Shalimov grins at the embarrassed Bassov.

Zamislov Varvara! We are planning a picnic, fair lady, a nautical picnic!

Yulia Yes, *and* we're going on a boat!

Varvara Come inside.

Zamislov Is Kaleria home?

Varvara, Zamislov and Yulia go inside. Suslov slowly gets up and follows them.

Shalimov (*chuckling*) Are we a little afraid of our lawful wedded wife, Sergei?

Bassov Not at all, not at all. She's a good companion, you know.

Shalimov Then why the note of sadness in your voice . . .?

Bassov (*under his breath, indicating Suslov*) Poor fellow's jealous. Of my assistant – see what I mean? Got it really bad. His wife . . . spellbinding woman . . .

At the far end of the clearing, Sonya and Zimin walk by.

Shalimov Is that so . . .?

Bassov Keep her under close observation.

Shalimov Normally I would do, but that Maria Lvovna has rather dampened my desire to charm the local talent.

Bassov This is a different case, old boy, altogether a different case! Take my word for it. (*Pause. They drink.*) Yakov, why is it so long since you've published? Got a major project under way?

Shalimov (*irritably*) No, I haven't got a major project under way. I haven't got a damn thing under way! Not written a word in years . . . How the devil can you write, when you don't understand what's going on in the world? Everything seems to be changing shape . . . slipping and sliding . . . nothing has any solidity!

Bassov Why don't you say that, then? 'I do not understand what's going on.' Isn't it crucial for a writer to have – above all else – sincerity?

Shalimov Oh, yes, thanks for reminding me. Jesus! If it had anything to do with sincerity, I would throw away my pen and grow cabbages, in the mode of Diocletian!

Bassov Ah. See what you mean.

A group of beggars appear out of the woods and slowly surround the Bassov dacha. During the dialogue, they chant:

Beggars Good people, give alms. Kind people, for the love of Christ, give alms. Good people, give a crust for the feast of Corpus Christi . . .

Neither Bassov nor Shalimov pays any attention to them.

Shalimov I need to eat. So I must write. But who am I writing for? It's a mystery. Five years ago I was quite convinced I knew my reader, knew what he was like, knew what he wanted from me. And then suddenly, overnight, I lost him. He simply disappeared! Catastrophe! Now they're saying a 'new reader' has emerged. A new reader! What the holy Jesus is that?

Bassov No, I don't follow. How can you have lost your reader? What about me, and all the fellows like me – we read you! Well, we buy them, anyway!

Pustobaika goes to the beggars and shoos them away. Kropilkin comes out of the woods and waves his rifle at them.

43

Shalimov Of course . . . loyal chaps. I appreciate it.

A beggar runs up to Bassov.

Beggar Alms for the hungry, kind Master.

Kropilkin runs up after him. Without really thinking, Bassov puts his hand in his pocket, finds a coin, and gives it to the beggar.

Bassov (*to Shalimov*) I still don't grasp the nature of the problem . . .

Kropilkin pulls the beggar away.

Kropilkin (*to Bassov*) Beg your pardon, sir.

Pustobaika and Kropilkin exit, herding off the beggars.

Shalimov Nor I, Sergei. But I feel it in my heart. I walk down the street, examining people – that's my job after all – and what I see I find profoundly shocking. There are certain physiognomies, certain alignments of tissue and bone, at which I look and think: These people are not going to read me! They quite simply don't give a damn! One evening last winter I made a rare public appearance, and a hundred pairs of eyes gazed up at me, attentive and curious, but somehow alien, misplaced, and it struck me that I was about as necessary to them as . . . Latin. These are the new readers. And I am ancient history. I can't figure it out. Who are they? What do they want?

Bassov A very tricky case, Yakov, very tricky. But maybe you're just feeling the pinch. Turbulent times and all that – half the country on strike – and yours is a highly demanding profession. Why not spend the summer here, have a drink and a laugh, settle your nerves . . . see what I mean? You'll find your reader again. One of the great lessons I've learned is that a calm and dignified attitude must be maintained, come what may. – Shall we go in?

They stand.

Oh, and Yakov . . . could you do something for me?
Could I ask you to . . . act the peacock a little?

Shalimov (*astonished*) Act the peacock? What the devil
do you mean?

Bassov I mean in front of my wife . . . Ruffle your tail
feathers, strut up and down like you used to . . . Varya
needs to be distracted. Something is eating at her.

Shalimov And I am to be the distraction? (*Laughs.*) Are
you out of your mind?

Bassov You agree?

Shalimov For an old friend . . . very well.

Bassov She's yearning for something. And I don't know
what. In fact, everyone in my circle's gone rather weird.
Moody. Talking in riddles. Very strange behaviour
altogether. By the way, did you get married again?

Shalimov Oh, yes. And divorced again, too. I tell you,
it's hard to make friends with women.

Bassov That's indubitably true.

*They go indoors. A lady in a yellow dress and a
young man in a check suit come out of the woods.*

Lady Isn't anyone here? Rehearsal was called for six
o'clock . . . That's typical of this company, that is!

Young Man I'm a romantic actor. I normally play the
juvenile lead. Only agreed to do this show as a favour to
the director.

Lady And what did he cast you as?

Young Man A pointless little comic turn. And under-
studying, of course. Absurd.

Lady I'm an understudy too. They give all the best parts to their friends!

Young Man Let's find the stage manager and complain.

They exit. Sonya and Zimin come out of the woods.

Sonya So it's goodbye. For three long weeks. You won't be back sooner?

Zimin No. Goodbye, my darling Sonya! You won't . . . whilst I'm away . . . you won't . . .

Sonya What?

Zimin Oh, no, I'm being weedy. Goodbye.

Sonya Say it. Whilst you're away, I won't . . .?

Zimin . . . Find someone else and fall instantly in love with them and get married and forget me?

Sonya I don't expect so, no. (*Laughs.*) Foolish boy! How can you say such things, Maxim? I've half a mind to be insulted.

Zimin Oh, don't be insulted! These crazy ideas come into my head . . . As they say, no man is completely in control of his emotions.

Sonya (*heatedly*) But we don't believe that, Max! You and I, we don't believe that! We know it's not true! It's just an excuse for weakness. Now go!

Zimin I'm going. I'll remember your words for ever! You are wonderful.

Zimin exits quickly. Sonya gazes after him, then goes on to the terrace and indoors. Dudakov, Vlass and Maria come out of the woods. Dvoetochie follows them.

Vlass My father was a cook. Potentially a very creative man. But he drank too hard. His love for me was

46

somewhat severe. So severe, I was dragged everywhere
he went. He had to travel to find work. Which meant his
marriage to my mother was . . . problematic. Once in a
while I'd run home to her, but he'd come steaming round
to the laundry, batter his way in, crack a few heads,
and put me back to work in the kitchens. Meanwhile he
developed the lethal notion that I should be educated.
This happened whilst he was working for a bishop, so
in short order I was installed in theological school. A
few months later, fired again, he went to work for the
railroad, so I found myself in technical college. Then it
was agriculture. Then art school, followed by business
administration, at which I proved less than a runaway
success, and was consequently thrashed. And put back
to work in the kitchens. To sum up: by the time I was
seventeen, I had such a deeply ingrained aversion to
learning anything at all, that even the rudiments of
smoking were beyond me. Why do you look at me like
that, Maria Lvovna?

Maria Because your story is sad.

Vlass Sad? Well, thankfully, it's ended.

*A servant woman with a bandaged face runs on,
breathless.*

Servant Oh, sir, oh, madam, have you seen a little boy?
He run away! Little Zenichka! Fair hair, only this high!
Have you seen him?

Maria No.

Servant Oh, God, he's run from the kitchen! They'll
thrash him when he's caught!

Vlass We said we haven't seen him.

Servant Zenichka!

She runs off.

47

Dvoetochie You know something, Vlass?

Vlass I know a lot of things.

Dvoetochie I like you.

Vlass Tell me more.

Dvoetochie That's it!

Vlass Well, I'm thrilled for you.

Dudakov (*to Vlass*) Your future is not looking very bright.

Vlass Which bit of my future?

Dudakov All of it.

Dvoetochie (*laughing*) No question, he'll have a miserable time. A straight man walks into the world, everyone else has a damn good laugh trying to make him bend. How long, do you think, before he knuckles under?

Vlass You'll have to wait and see, won't you? – They're probably serving tea. Shall we go in?

Dudakov (*consults his watch*) Yes, ah, there's just time.

Dvoetochie I could drink a glass of tea. Do you think anyone would mind?

Vlass Come as my guest, old man. I'll just run ahead and check.

Vlass runs into the dacha. The others follow slowly.

Dvoetochie He's not a bad lad.

Maria No, he isn't. Such a pity he's so affected . . .

Dvoetochie That's nothing. It'll pass. Deep down inside, he's honest. Most people wear their honesty tacked on like a medal. You can hear the buggers shout: I'm honest! I'm honest! But it's like this: the more a young girlie goes around insisting she's a virgin, the more you can be sure she's joined the club! (*He roars with laughter.*) You'll have to forgive me, Maria Lvovna.

Maria It's about what I expected.

They go up on to the terrace. They meet Suslov coming out.

Dvoetochie Where are you off to, Pyotr?

Suslov Oh, just for a smoke . . . get some air . . .

Dvoetochie, Maria and Dudakov go inside. Suslov lights a cigarette. The servant woman with a bandaged face runs up to him, panting.

Servant Oh, sir, have you seen a little serving boy? I've got to find him quick!

Suslov (*quietly*) Piss off.

The servant woman runs away. A man in a top hat passes her as he comes out of the woods. He bows extravagantly to Suslov.

Top Hat A very good evening, sir. I dare say you're looking for me?

Suslov I'm not looking for anybody. She was. I'm not.

Top Hat We can ignore the mix-up. I've been cast, don't you know, in the lead.

Suslov What?

Top Hat In the play!

Suslov (*walking away*) I don't give a shit.

Top Hat (*running after him*) But allow me to ask, sir – who does? Where might one find the director? *Is* there a director? I've been entirely alone for two hours!

Suslov evades him.

(*Pouts.*) Philistine.

> *The man in a top hat goes off behind the stage. Suslov meets Olga coming along the path from the Suslov dacha.*

Olga Hello, Pyotr.

Suslov Good evening. Sultry weather.

Olga Sultry? No.

Suslov Well, I'm suffocating. I say, there are a bunch of maniacs tearing about, looking for serving boys . . . directors . . . it's insanity . . .

Olga Are you all right? You're shaking.

> *Suslov walks back with her towards the Bassov dacha.*

Suslov I drank too much last night.

Olga Why do you do it?

Suslov Well, if you felt like I do in the morning, *you'd* need a drink.

Olga Have you seen my husband?

Suslov He's at the Bassovs'.

> *Varvara comes out on to the terrace.*

Varvara Coming in to see me, Olga?

Olga Just taking a stroll.

Varvara (*to Suslov*) And why did you leave us?

Suslov Because I'm heartily sick of listening to speeches. Mr Russian Literature holding forth. And Maria Red-Flag Lvovna.

Varvara Don't you find it informative? I do.

Suslov (*shrugs*) That's up to you. Goodnight.

Suslov exits towards his dacha.

Olga (*quietly*) Well. Have you any idea why he's like that?

Varvara No. Nor do I wish to. Coming in?

Olga Stay outside with me. They'll manage without you.

Varvara I'm sure. – You seem flustered again.

Olga How could I not be? He dashes back from town, spends two minutes with the children, then dashes out again! Hardly guaranteed to make me leap for joy, is it?

They wander towards the trees.

Varvara He's at our house.

Olga He's running away from family life, that's what he's doing. I know, I know, he's overworked, he needs a break, but what about me? Don't I get a break? I work myself into the ground! And nothing I can do or say is right. Lord! It makes me livid! He needs reminding that I've sacrificed my youth, my looks, everything – all for him!

Varvara (*gently*) Dear Olga . . . you do like a moan, don't you?

From indoors comes the sound of an argument, increasing in volume.

Olga Well, what if I do? I feel I should say to him: I'm going away! Taking the children and going away!

Varvara That's a splendid idea. Give yourselves a rest from each other. Make the arrangements, I'll lend you the money.

Olga I owe you too much already!

Varvara It's nothing. Let's try and calm down a little. Come, sit.

Ryumin crosses at the rear, on his way to the Bassov dacha.

Olga I hate myself for not being able to manage without your help. Do you think I like taking your husband's money? How can one have any self-respect, if one can't manage the household finances . . . can't get by without hand-outs? Well? Well? Do you know there are times when I don't like you? Loathe you in fact. Can't bear you. Always so calm and rational. Never showing any real *passion*!

Varvara But my dear, it's my way of coping. I simply don't allow myself to complain. It doesn't mean I don't feel like it!

Olga I believe that those who are always helping others must, at the bottom of their hearts, despise the ones they're helping. Yes. And I'd like to be one of the helpers.

Varvara So you can despise the needy?

Olga Yes! Yes! I don't like people! Why should I like people? I don't like Maria Lvovna – who does she think she is, to judge us from on high? I don't like Ryumin. Spouts his philosophy, hasn't the guts to lift a finger. Do you think I like your husband? He's as soft as bread before you put it in the oven. And he's petrified of you. That's a great example, that is! And as for your brother, who's in love with the shrew Lvovna –

Varvara (*surprised*) Olga! What has come over you? That's not nice at all!

Olga So? And Kaleria – arrogant hussy. Claims to be searching for truth and beauty – really looking for a man to take her to bed!

Varvara Olga! Stop this! You shouldn't allow yourself to . . . These are dark places, Olga, dark!

Olga (*softly, but maliciously*) I do not care. I do not care where we go, as long as it's away from here, this unendurable drudgery! I want to live! I'm no worse than anyone else! I've got eyes in my head, I'm not thick! I can see that even you – oh, you live very nicely thank you, your husband's made some money – not a hundred per cent honestly, either, according to what people say – you've contrived – somehow – not to tie yourself down with screaming children!

Varvara stands and stares at Olga, completely amazed.

Varvara Contrived . . .? What are you implying?

Olga I don't know how you did it!

Varvara (*very coldly*) Did what? What do you mean?

Pause. Olga begins to squirm with embarrassment.

Olga Not anything in particular . . . but my husband says . . . some women don't want children.

Varvara I have no idea what you actually think. But you clearly suspect me of something base. Don't say any more.

Olga Varya, I didn't mean it . . . Don't look at me like that . . . I'm only repeating what everyone knows about your husband . . .

Varvara I have treated you as my sister. If I didn't know how difficult things are for you . . . If I didn't know how we used to dream, to share our dreams of another way of life . . . Oh, God!

Olga I've said something awful, haven't I? Please, please forgive me. I'm so nasty!

Varvara We've watched our dreams disintegrate, wept for them together. I'm very hurt, Olga. Have you got what you wanted? (*Yells.*) You hurt me!

Olga Don't be like that, Varya!

Varvara I'm going.

Varvara moves away. Olga gets up too.

Don't follow me. Don't you dare follow me!

Olga What, never? Can't I be with you, ever? Varya?

Varvara I don't understand! Why have you done this to me?

Dvoetochie scuttles down from the terrace towards them.

Dvoetochie I've escaped! Take me by the hand, beautiful.

He takes Varvara's hand.

That world renowned thinker Ryumin got me in an awful muddle. It's all too subtle for an old goat like me. Normally I'd sort it out with a quick one-two, but I got bogged down in his speeches like a beetle in syrup . . . My head's spinning . . . So I simply ran away! Brilliant, eh? They can all go to blazes! I'll have a gossip with you. You're all right, you are. – But what's this? You haven't been crying . . .?

Dvoetochie looks at Olga, looks back at Varvara, gets the picture, and is embarrassed.

Olga (*meekly*) Do you want me to go, Varvara?

Varvara Yes.

Olga creeps away and exits.

I'm sorry. What were you saying?

Dvoetochie Oh, my dear friend . . .! Have you had some trouble? You're like a fish out of water, you know that? A pretty little flatfish, gasping for air . . .

Varvara Would you mind telling me, Mr Dvoetochie, what you think gives you the right to address me like that?

Dvoetochie (*laughs*) I'm old, that's all! I'm so old I'm practically dead! When you reach my age you can get away with murder.

Varvara Forgive me, but I'm not sure that's sufficient . . . You barge in so gracelessly . . .

Dvoetochie (*good-naturedly*) I don't barge in, sweetheart, I sort of sidle up – expertise, see – on account of I don't belong here either. I'm gasping for air just like you. That's what I'm trying to say. But I haven't the words to put it all sissy and clever.

Varvara (*softening*) Oh, I don't mind really. Don't think me rude. I'm just not used to this kind of behaviour.

Dvoetochie You've never been to Siberia, have you? Come on, take me for a walk. Humour an old goat!

Varvara It's turning chilly. Let me fetch my shawl, and we'll go.

> *Varvara goes inside. Semyonov comes belting in on a bicycle, and crashes to a halt at Dvoetochie's feet.*

Semyonov Sorry I'm late, had a puncture!

Dvoetochie Where do you think you're going at such dangerous speed, you idiot?

Semyonov The others are on their way! Two girls, and a cadet! They'll be here any moment. They know their lines – at least I think they do!

Dvoetochie I'm glad to hear it. Who are these people again?

Semyonov You know, the cadet whose sister shot herself! And the two girls are just – well, girls, really!

Dvoetochie I'd be very happy to meet them. But why would they want to meet me?

Semyonov You're in the cast, aren't you?

Dvoetochie Not as far as I know. I'm about to take a walk with a captivating lady.

Semyonov An actress?

Dvoetochie Certainly not.

Semyonov So you aren't . . .? This isn't the . . .?

Dvoetochie I assure you I'm not in a play, young feller.

Semyonov Oh, heck! I'm frightfully sorry! It's just – with the wig, and the make-up – I assumed you were some sort of character actor.

Dvoetochie (*forcefully*) I am not wearing a wig.

Semyonov Come off it, yes you are!

Dvoetochie I'm nothing to do with your amateur dramatics!

Semyonov What are you, then? The props man?

The woman in a yellow dress and the young man in a check suit come out from behind the stage.

Woman Semyonov!

Young Man Over here!

Suslov comes down the path from his dacha.

Semyonov Oh, there they are! (*to Dvoetochie*) You know, the make-up's a good idea. Everybody looks better in make-up!

Semyonov wheels his bike over towards the stage.

Much better than in real life!

Dvoetochie Holy God.

Suslov approaches him.

Suslov Seen my wife?

Dvoetochie shakes his head.

The dacha is swarming with actors. They say she invited
them!

Dvoetochie Actors! Who can tolerate 'em? Why we give
them space on the bloody earth, I've no idea.

*From the Bassov dacha come Kaleria, Shalimov,
Ryumin and Varvara, locked in debate.*

Strewth, they're still at it . . .

*Dvoetochie goes over to listen to them. Suslov sits
with his head in his hands.*

Shalimov I tell you, I'd happily traverse the Arctic Circle
just to avoid her. She's impossibly hot-tempered!

Ryumin It makes me furious, that level of didacticism!
These types are criminally intolerant! Why do they
assume we should agree with everything they say?

Varvara Show them something finer, then. More
impressive dreams.

Kaleria There's nothing impressive about her dreams.
Equitable redistribution of wealth. Welfare for the poor,
work for the work-shy. Democracy! (*Groans.*) Cold and
unpoetic, her dreams.

Varvara But I've yet to hear anything more exciting! I'm
not very eloquent, I know, but surely, my good friends,
we have a duty to encourage people to believe in themselves! To recognise their value, to recover their dignity!
Only then can we begin to behave like human beings!
Surely!

Kaleria Dear God, I don't think Maria Lvovna's the one to teach us how to behave like human beings!

Varvara But why do you all dislike her so?

Ryumin First, because she's Maria Lvovna. Second, because she's the most exasperating person any of us have ever met. When someone insists to me that they alone know the true meaning of life, I feel as if I'm being pinioned by some desperate creature, maimed and mutilated, crushed underfoot!

Kaleria The society of such people is asphyxiating.

Varvara And the society of people who do nothing but grumble – is that freer, Kaleria? Be fair to her – it can't be positive to live among those who only worry about themselves, can it? Those who fill their life with complaint, but contribute precisely nothing? What do we – you, me, you, you – what do we contribute? What?

Ryumin And what does she contribute? Pure aggression.

Kaleria And empty words. Her politics are out of date – out of place in the new Russia.

Varvara No, it's not so!

Over by the stage, the amateur actors start to gather. Pustobaika enters, helping with the scenery.

Dvoetochie Mrs Bassova, don't let a lot of speechifying upset you. It's all manure, in the end. Come and have a walk, like you promised.

Varvara Yes, I shall. I wish I could express myself more clearly! It's infuriating, being so unintelligent.

Shalimov I assure you, that you are not. Would you mind if I join you?

Varvara nods her assent.

Dvoetochie We'll go to the river and sit in the summer-house, shall we?

Varvara, Dvoetochie and Shalimov head off through the woods. Ryumin and Kaleria turn to each other and smile.

Ryumin Well, she's certainly perked up since Shalimov arrived. Fiery words, eh? And for what? Some burnt-out hack who can no longer feel the earth beneath his feet . . . Do you know how to tell when he's lying?

Kaleria How?

Ryumin His lips move.

Kaleria She knows what he's like. She talked to him last night. I saw her later. Crying like a baby. Disappoint-ment . . . I suppose he looked so mighty from afar. She thought he'd put some sparkle in her barren little life.

Zamislov and Yulia come around the corner of the Bassov dacha. He whispers to her, and she giggles. Suslov watches them.

Ryumin Will you play something for me? I'd like that.

Kaleria Yes. When the world is so sad, we need music.

Ryumin and Kaleria go inside.

Yulia Oh, goody – actors! What time did you call the rehearsal?

Zamislov Six.

Yulia What time is it now?

Zamislov Half-past seven.

Yulia We're late!

Zamislov Well, everyone expects you to be late. But now I'm late too. That's your bad influence.

Yulia Are you being impertinent?

Zamislov No, no, complimentary. I'd rather have a bad influence than a good any day.

Yulia laughs happily.

I have to pay a quick call on my boss, if you'll permit me.

Yulia Don't be long!

Zamislov goes into the Bassov dacha. Yulia walks towards the stage, and sees Suslov.

Suslov Where have you been?

Yulia Here and there.

By the stage are the lady in a yellow dress, the young man in a check suit, the man in a top hat, Semyonov, the cadet and the two girls. Pustobaika struggles with the scenery. Laughter and chatter, as they await Zamislov's arrival.

Suslov With him? And so publicly? Don't you see what a spectacle you're making of yourself? People are laughing at me, Yulia!

Yulia Laughing at *you*? Never.

Suslov We need to have a heart-to-heart. I cannot allow you to become –

Yulia The wife of a man people laugh at? No, doesn't suit me, either.

Suslov Be careful, Yulia! You don't know what I'm capable of.

Yulia Yes I do. You're capable of behaving like a drunken pig. I know that.

Suslov Don't you speak to me in that manner, you little whore! You are depraved!

Yulia (*calmly*) If you want to have a scene, let's have it at home. My supporting cast are over there. I don't want you embarrassing me in front of them. You with your blotchy red face.

Suslov takes a step towards her and raises his hand. She stands her ground. He backs off quickly.

Suslov I'll shoot you one day.

Yulia I'm free on Tuesday if that's any good.

Suslov exits through the woods.

(*Sings softly.*)
The sun sinks wearily
Into a blood-red sea . . .

Her voice falters. She exits a different way from Suslov. Maria Lvovna, very agitated, and Dudakov and Bassov, carrying fishing rods, come out of the Bassov dacha. Bassov is trying to untangle his line.

Bassov Damnation, who got my line all tangled? (*to Maria*) You ought to go a little easier on folks, you know.

Maria I beg your pardon!

Dudakov People get tired, d'you see?

Bassov It's just not acceptable. By your rule-book, if a chap becomes a writer, he must automatically become some sort of hero, too. But it isn't the case. Not all writers have it in them.

Maria Everyone should push themselves harder.

Bassov Oh, goes without saying, perpetual self-improvement – all for it, aren't we, Kirill? But there are limits to what's possible.

Dudakov Ah, limits, yes, there are limits.

Bassov If you want to achieve something, you go about it gradually, see what I mean? Evolution is the byword here. That's one of the great lessons I've learned. Evolution is the way forward.

Maria I am not demanding the impossible. We live in a country where, given the nature of the body politic, the writer, and only the writer, can become a spokesman for truth and decency. Do we have a free press? Do we have a forum for debate? No. Who speaks for the people? No-one. Only the writer can become an impartial judge of our vices, and a fighter for our rights. Therefore, that's what the Russian writer must be. There's no argument.

Bassov You're quite right. None the less . . .

Maria And is your friend like that? Not a bit of it! What's he searching for? What are his ideals? Who is he, my friend? Or my enemy? It's like his identity's been surgically removed. I haven't an inkling who he is!

Maria exits quickly. Bassov is still struggling with his line.

Bassov I've the utmost admiration for your revolutionary zeal, but . . . Has she gone? Phew. What was she so steamed up about?

Dudakov . . . Ah . . . couldn't say.

Bassov Every schoolboy knows an author's supposed to champion great causes and lay bare the unpalatable facts and scourge the powers-that-be and so on, but this mule of a woman has to ram it down our throats till we're blue in the face. Good God above! Let's go and catch some fish.

Dudakov Easy for her to be smart. Got her own practice. Works when she likes.

Bassov Notice how Yakov wriggled out of it when she put him on the spot? Sly as a fox, he is. (*Chuckles.*) Only spent six months living with his last wife before he ditched her –

Dudakov The polite word is 'divorced'.

Bassov Divorced, ditched, whatever – anyway, now she's dead he's trying to claim her inheritance! Nice little estate in the Ukraine. Got some balls or what?

Dudakov That's, ah, on the greedy side, wouldn't you say?

Bassov Greedy? Hardly the case. You can never have too much property.

Dudakov (*thoughtfully*) I find it remarkable . . .

Bassov What?

Dudakov That we don't all loathe each other.

Bassov You serious?

Dudakov Entirely. Fact is, we are – what is the phrase – hollow men? Are we not?

Bassov Speak for yourself, Doctor! All my essential organs are *in situ*. I'm in the prime of life!

Dudakov Don't be, ah, flippant, Sergei. I feel quite empty inside.

Bassov Physician, heal thyself, is all I can say to that! Right, let's go. You won't push me in the river, will you?

Dudakov Why the dickens would I?

Bassov Well, you're in a very odd mood.

They head off.

Dudakov You know, it's damned hard to have an adult conversation with you.

Bassov Then don't waste your breath, if you see what I mean. It's not compulsory.

They exit through the woods. Zamislov comes out of the dacha, runs hurriedly to the stage, and starts addressing the actors, who greet him noisily. Meanwhile Sonya and Vlass enter.

Sonya But I'm not convinced you have any poetic talent.

Vlass Ah, there you're wrong. I've talent coming out of my toenails. How about this:

Here is a peach. Here is a pineapple.
Food for the wealthy, but not for Vlass.
In all his days, he never shall grapple
With such exotic fruits – alas!

Sonya (*laughs*) Why do you waste your time on such tosh? Why not have a go at something proper?

Vlass Oh, Sonya, brainy little Sonya, I have struggled with profundity, struggled and strained, and this is all I came up with:

I'm too clever for art
And too dim to be smart.

Sonya (*seriously*) Vlass, I don't believe you. I don't believe you're that superficial. Tell me what you really want.

Vlass What do I want? (*Thinks.*) I want to live well.

Sonya And what are you doing about it?

Vlass Nothing.

Maria (*off*) Sonya!

Sonya Here, Mama!

Maria Your guests have arrived!

Maria Lvovna enters.

Better go home.

Sonya Off I fly . . .! I'll hand this ventriloquist over to you. If he talks gibberish, punch him.

Sonya exits.

Vlass (*stupid peasant voice*) I 'on't talk no gibrudge, Missus. I ony bin a-tryin' a kermoonicate wi' that whelp o' yourn on moi way back from railway station.

Maria (*gently*) Vlass, dear, why do you do it? You debase yourself. What is the point?

Vlass The point? I like to hear people laughing. If I'm not funny, they don't. (*suddenly very serious*) I'm sick of it, Maria. Downright sick. It's not as if they're people I love. Or respect. Or find any value in. They're tiny, insignificant things . . . mosquitoes . . . You can't *talk* to them. They're so stupid, I feel a grotesque need to be even stupider. My head's crammed with all their bilge. I want sometimes to drown it in vodka! I don't know how to live amongst them and yet be different from them. It's poisoning me. This banality . . .

We hear voices, off.

Listen, they're coming. Christ, how it fills me with horror! Take me away somewhere, will you? I'm so hungry for your conversation!

Maria (*taking his arm*) If you knew how happy it makes me, to hear you talk like this . . .

Exit Vlass and Maria into the woods. Enter Shalimov, Yulia and Varvara.

Shalimov Stop, stop, I can't take any more! Have mercy on a poor author! I've had quite enough theorising for today. Couldn't I just vegetate for a while? Lie down, let my roots soak up some moisture? I don't really want to do anything more stressful than flirting with beautiful women.

Yulia You don't find flirting stressful? In that case, why aren't you flirting with me?

Shalimov I shall take you up on your invitation.

Yulia It wasn't an invitation, it was an academic point.

Shalimov Academic or not, sounded like an invitation to me.

Yulia Well, you carry on in your own little world, Mr Shalimov. I'm still waiting to hear your opinion.

Shalimov My opinion. Very well. Friendship between a man and a woman is an – academic – possibility, yet it will, inevitably, die. Biological realities, d'you see, intrude.

Yulia In other words, it can only exist as a prelude to love?

Shalimov Ah, now, love, I tell you – now we're on to something *truly* serious. When I love a woman, I want to lift her off the earth, high off the earth, and array her in the cornucopia of my inspiration . . .!

Zamislov (*calls from the stage*) Yulia! On stage, please!

Yulia Time for my entrance! Goodbye, Mr Fruit-and-Veg man! Don't let your roots get waterlogged.

Yulia goes to the stage.

Shalimov Vivacious little creature . . .! Why do you look at me like that, Varvara?

Varvara It's the moustache. It suits you.

Shalimov You think so? A thousand thanks. But I have the suspicion you disapprove of . . . Some women, I find, can only converse in a certain language. You are shocked?

Varvara Not much shocks me any more.

Shalimov Understood. Nevertheless, you think me equivocal. Well, we can't all be as blunt as that hysterical Mr Ryumin. – Oh, I'm sorry. He's your friend.

Varvara I have no friends.

Shalimov I value the inner machinery of my psyche far too highly to open it up for inspection. The secrets of Pythagoras were only revealed to the chosen few.

Varvara I think I've gone off your moustache.

Shalimov What the devil's the moustache got to do with it? You know the saying, when in Rome . . . I admit to a touch of the chameleon. When you have drunk the cup of loneliness, you may feel the same. Until then, don't let me detain you.

He bows and walks over to the stage, where an audience is gathering. Zamislov, prompt-book in hand, is directing Semyonov. Bassov hurries on with his fishing rod.

Bassov Varya! I've been in fishing heaven! What do you make of this?

He produces a fish from his bag. Varvara screws up her nose.

Even Dudakov, who can barely cast, landed a couple! (*Glances around.*) Look here, dearest. On my way up the path from the river, I happened to glance into the trees, and do you know what I saw? I saw Vlass, on his knees, in front of Maria Lvovna. And the boy was kissing her hands! I mean, good God! She's old enough to be his mother! Will you have a word with him?

Varvara (*urgently*) Sergei, listen a minute. Keep it to yourself. Don't breathe a word! I'm sure you've misread the situation. It would be terrible to –

Bassov Keep your hair on! I won't tell. But Maria Lvovna . . . good God!

Varvara Sergei, promise me! Promise!

Bassov Oh, to hell with them both – I promise! But what's going on?

Varvara I don't know what's going on. But it's not what you think. They're not having an affair!

Bassov Oh, they're not, eh? What was she doing, then? Brushing his teeth? But I went fishing and I didn't see a thing. Just fish, that's all I saw. (*He chortles.*) I say, have you heard about Yakov? Isn't he a swine?

Varvara (*in despair*) What now?

Bassov Why are you so touchy? This is a different story!

Varvara I don't want to know any more stories. Can't you get it into your head? I don't want to know!

Bassov You are weird. It's nothing spectacular. Yakov's asked me to represent him when he goes to court over his late wife's –

Varvara I'm begging you! I'm begging you! Be quiet!

Bassov (*offended*) I will if I may suggest that we seek some medication for you, Varya. For your nerves. It's getting beyond a joke. Do you see what I mean?

Bassov goes into the dacha. Varvara stays on the terrace. There is commotion around the stage.

Zamislov Watchman!

Pustobaika Yes sir?

Zamislov Where's the lantern?

Yulia Where's my script?

Semyonov Can I make a cut just here?

Zamislov Quiet! Quiet!

Lady I can't possibly wear this hat!

Yulia (*voice exercises*) La la la la!

Zamislov Quiet, please! Attention, ladies and gentlemen! Act One, Scene One – beginners! The play is about to commence!

Yulia bursts into song.
End of Act Two.

Act Three

A clearing in the woods. At the rear, under the trees,
Bassov, Suslov, Shalimov and Dvoetochie laze on a rug,
surrounded by empty bottles. To one side there is a
samovar; nearby, Sasha is washing dishes. Pustobaika
lies down, smoking his pipe. Beside him are oars and a
bucket. Further off, Sonya is sitting with two young
musicians, who have a guitar and a mandolin. Towards
the front, Kaleria, Varvara and Yulia sit on bales of
straw.

   It's late afternoon. Bassov tells a joke to the men in a
low voice. The musicians strum gently. Yulia yawns.

Yulia Boring picnic.

Kaleria Boring life.

Varvara The men are having fun.

Yulia They've had plenty to drink. Now they'll be
swapping dirty stories.

   Pause.

Sonya (*to the musicians*) A little more slowly . . .

   Pause. Dvoetochie laughs.

Yulia Had a few drinks myself. Didn't make me very
merry. Wine, actually, makes me feel worse. Makes the
living that bit harder . . . I get this urge to do something
wild.

Kaleria It's all so unclear . . . blurry round the edges . . .
frightens me.

Varvara What frightens you?

Kaleria I don't feel I can trust anyone. They're all so unreliable.

Varvara Yes . . . They are, aren't they?

Bassov And she turns to him and she says: 'I only come in for a sausage.'

The men laugh.

Dvoetochie (*getting up*) Very good.

Varvara (*to Kaleria*) I do understand you.

Kaleria No you don't, don't begin to think so. You don't understand me, I don't understand you, nobody understands anyone. We drift about like ice-floes in the Baltic . . . banging into each other . . .

Dvoetochie exits.

Yulia (*sings, softly*)
The sun sinks wearily
Into a blood-red sea . . .

Varvara It's becoming more and more like a meat-market, the way we live. Everyone wants to get as much as they can for as little as possible.

Yulia (*sings*)
Indigo skies grow darker
Shadows mantle me . . .

Kaleria What would make people more bearable, do you think?

Varvara Honesty.

Kaleria Honesty? No. Conviction.

Yulia I wish you two would give up. It's not the most amusing repartee I've ever heard.

Varvara You sing superbly, Yulia.

Yulia I love music more than anything.

Kaleria I don't even love that any more. I don't think I can love at all. There are big black clouds inside me. An angry storm about to break.

Varvara My dear, that's too depressing . . .

Kaleria I shall die unmarried.

Yulia It's not all it's cracked up to be, let me assure you! I suppose you could always marry Ryumin.

Kaleria Ryumin? The india-rubber man?

Sonya (*to the musicians*) All set? Mandolin first, then you come in.

The musicians play. The women listen.

Varvara Reminds me of a song the washerwomen used to sing, in the place where my mother worked. I think I'd just started school. I remember the laundry full of grey steam, and half-dressed women, singing in tired voices:

Mother, pity me
Your poor little girl.
Crying among strangers
Alone in the world.

Used to make me weep, that song.

Bassov Sasha! Bring some more beer!

Sasha takes beer to the men.

Varvara I had a good life then . . .! Those rough women loved me. When they'd finished work in the evenings, they used to drink tea at a long, scrubbed pine table – and they'd sit me down among them, as if I was grown-up, too.

Kaleria How dreary. You're as bad as Maria Lvovna.

Yulia The way we live now is despicable . . .

Varvara Yes, it is. And we've no idea how to live better. My mother slaved for forty years, yet you can't conceive how generous she was! And how cheerful! Everybody adored her. She pushed me to study – I remember her utter joy when I graduated from college. She could barely walk by that time. Rheumatism. And when she died she said, 'Don't cry, Varya. It's nothing. You live, you work, and then it's time to go.' I think there was a lot more meaning to her life than there is to mine. I feel clumsy and ignorant, a stranger in a strange land, out of my depth. I don't understand the world in which cultured people live. It seems so brittle, knocked together fast like booths at the fair. No, like ice fragments floating on a river . . . they gleam and glitter, but they're riddled with dirt, with shame . . . Whenever I read a really honest, straightforward book, a courageous book, it's as if the sun is rising, a light of truth in the sky, and it will melt the filthy ice, and the pure, clean water will wash it away . . .

Kaleria Why don't you leave your husband?

Varvara stares at her in bewilderment.

He's so vulgar. Superfluous to requirements. Leave him, go off, study! Work! Fall in love!

Varvara (*stands, annoyed*) You are too crude.

Kaleria Squalor doesn't bother you, you've lived among washerwomen. You could live anywhere!

Yulia That's your own brother you're talking about.

Kaleria It can be your husband if you like.

Yulia Suits me. (*Laughs.*) I doubt I'll get upset. I frequently tell him what I think of him, which of course drives him mad. Then he has his turn. The other day he said I was depraved.

73

Varvara (*shocked*) What did you do?

Yulia Nothing. What's the point in arguing? I'm not entirely sure what depraved means, but I've a jolly good mind to find out. It's presumably to do with men. And that's a subject which intrigues me . . . I know I'm pretty. Just my rotten luck. Whilst I was still at school the masters began to stare . . . and I'd blush . . . and they'd leer and grin like gluttons in a pie-shop.

Kaleria Oh, how disgusting.

Yulia Yes, it was. I confided in friends who'd got married, and they enlightened me. But I've my darling husband to thank for arousing me to such a peak of curiosity. He's the one who managed to really corrupt my imagination. (*Laughs.*) So in return I corrupt his life. Fair exchange, they say, is no robbery.

Shalimov approaches them.

Shalimov One of my favourite proverbs! Quoted it many a time! – Varvara, would you care to stroll by the river?

Varvara Yes, I wouldn't mind.

Shalimov May I offer you my arm?

Varvara (*firmly*) No, thank you.

They move away from the others.

Shalimov You're a sad little thing. Not at all like your brother. He's the life and soul of the party, he is.

They exit.

Kaleria No-one we know is contented. Even you – always sunny – but underneath . . .

Yulia Do you like that man? I think he's a fake. Cold skin, like a frog. Let's go down to the river, too!

Kaleria Let's! (*standing*) Why not?

Yulia I've a feeling he's soft on her. But she's so remote! I'm fond of Varya, but afraid of her, too. Far too pure for my taste.

They exit to the river. There are shouts, off: 'Use the boat!' 'Grab it!' 'Where are the oars?' 'We need oars!' Pustobaika puts out his pipe, gets up slowly, and lifts the oars on to his shoulders. Bassov and Suslov go off towards the noise. Sasha follows them off, as do Sonya and the musicians. Zamislov runs on and grabs the oars from Pustobaika.

Zamislov Get a move on, you old snail! Got wax in your ears? There'll be a drowning in a minute, and you stand around like a bloody scarecrow!

He runs off with the oars. Pustobaika follows at his own pace.

Pustobaika (*to himself*) Drowning? They don't shout like that when they's drowning. Anyhow, you be a hero, sonny – all the fucking same to me . . .

He exits. The stage is empty for a few seconds. We hear further shouts: 'Don't throw rocks at it!' 'They'll capsize!' 'Give them the oars!' Then laughter.
Vlass and Maria Lvovna enter from a different direction.

Maria You mustn't say that, I won't allow it!

Vlass I will say it. I will!

Maria You must treat me with respect!

Vlass But I love you! I love you! I'm out of my mind with it, I love the way you think, the way you look, the lock of grey hair that gets in your eyes.

Maria Be quiet, you be quiet!

Vlass I need you! Like air to breathe! I cannot live without you!

Maria Oh my God – we can't do this, can we?

Vlass You've given me back my self-esteem. I was in darkness. Walking off the path. You've shown me how to be a man.

Maria You're torturing me! My darling, go away!

Vlass (*on his knees*) You've given me so much. But I beg you to be generous – give more!

Maria I beg *you* – leave me alone!

Vlass Tell me you can love me back!

Maria Later . . . I'll answer later . . . I'm an old woman! Can't you see? I insist that you stop this instantly, Vlass, and leave me, go away!

Vlass I'll go. And you'll tell me later?

Maria Later! Later! Yes!

> *Vlass exits quickly, almost colliding with Varvara, who gives him one of her looks.*

Varya . . .

Varvara What is it? Has he been horrible?

Maria No . . . Yes! Horrible? I don't know! I don't understand!

Varvara Come, come, sit down . . .! Tell me what happened.

Maria He said . . . (*She looks at Varvara, confused.*) He said he loves me! But I have grey hair! And three false teeth! Surely he can see that? My daughter is eighteen!

Varvara Oh my darling! Try not to cry . . . You are a . . .

Maria What? I'm a what? I'm an unhappy woman, that's what I am! Help me to get rid of him!

Varvara I see, you feel pity, but not love . . .

Maria Oh, no!

Sonya comes on silently and stands behind them. She holds flowers in her hands, intending to scatter them over Maria. Instead, she listens.

Varvara Poor Vlassik . . .!

Maria No, no, you've got it wrong! It's not pity for him! It's pity for me!

Varvara But why?

Maria Because I love him. (*Pause. She snuffles.*) Does that seem absurd? Yes, I love him. Grey hair and all. I'm hungry for it. Hungry for life!

Sonya exits silently.

I don't feel I've lived at all, yet. My marriage was a sham. Three years. I've never known love. And now – ashamed though I am to admit it – I'm desperate for some tenderness . . . some comfort . . . But it's a bit late, don't you think? You have to help me, Varya. Persuade him he's made a mistake . . . that he doesn't love me . . . that it was all a dream. I think I've been tortured enough.

Varvara My dear friend . . .! What are you so afraid of? If you genuinely love each other . . .?

Maria . . . You actually think it's realistic? What about Sonya? And my age, my damned age? Won't he leave me after a year? I couldn't bear the humiliation!

Varvara You can't calculate everything! The odds for this, the odds against that. Don't be scared to live! You deserve some happiness. And you could do so much for my brother . . . He never really had a mother, and goodness, how he's suffered . . .

Maria (*bowing her head*) A mother . . . yes. Just a mother. I understand now. Thank you.

Varvara No, you mistake me, that wasn't to say –

Ryumin comes out of the woods, sees the women, and stops.

Maria I know you didn't mean to. But you hit on a simple truth. I should be a mother to him. That's what I should be. A friend. I have to leave you now, I have to cry.

She stands, and sees Ryumin.

I'll bet I look a sight. – Yes, the old bitch has finally flipped.

Maria exits wearily. Ryumin approaches Varvara.

Varvara I'll come with you.

Ryumin Varvara – a moment –

Varvara (*to Maria*) I'll catch you up! (*to Ryumin*) What is it?

Ryumin Wait! Wait.

He glances round, seeming to hear something.

Varvara Why are you being so mysterious?

Suslov crosses the back of the stage, and exits.

Ryumin (*checks the coast is clear*) Now. At once. – You've known me a long time.

Varvara Four years, I think, but –

Ryumin For a long time now . . . For a long time, I've wanted to say . . . Varya, surely you know what I'm getting at!

Varvara frowns at him and moves away. Pause.

Varvara What a strange day . . .!

Ryumin I feel I've loved you all my life . . . Before I even knew you . . . You were the woman of my dreams, the dreams one conjures in one's youth, the picture of an ideal love . . . You can search for ever, and maybe never find it . . . But I have met my dream.

Varvara Pavel, I prefer you not to talk like this. I don't love you at all.

Ryumin But can I just say –

Varvara No. Why?

Ryumin (*laughs quietly*) So that's over and done with. How clinical, in the end. I've been building up to it for such a long, long time . . . anticipating with both dread and pleasure the moment when I'd steel myself to say . . . I love you. And there we are. I've said it.

Varvara But Pavel – what do you expect me to do?

Ryumin Oh, naturally I see your predicament. But all my hopes rested in you. And now all hope is gone. I'm a dead man.

Varvara Don't talk like that! Don't punish me! I'm not to blame!

Ryumin I'm the one who's being punished! I'm the walking example of unfulfilled promise. When I was young, I made such vows . . .! To struggle for all that was right and true! My best years are behind me – and I've done nothing. Waited too long for the perfect moment. Got accustomed to a life of ease.

79

Varvara But –

Ryumin Please, allow me my little confession. I no longer want your love. I simply want you to feel sorry for me. Life terrifies me – it makes such demands! One throws up a smokescreen of abstraction . . . When I met you, a pure, bright hope burnt in my heart, that you would lend me the strength to fulfil my vows, to create a better world!

Varvara But I can't put my blood in your veins! There is no power that can regenerate a person from outside. It's either in you or it's not. – I won't say any more. I'm beginning to feel hostile.

Ryumin Towards me? Why?

Varvara Oh, not just you . . . towards everyone. We are like aliens on this earth. We don't know how to be useful. New people will come soon – maybe tomorrow – bold, strong creatures, quite different from us, they will take one look at us, they will see how useless we are, and they will sweep us off the planet like trash. Our hideous lies – they're what I'm hostile towards.

Ryumin But I like my lies! Without them, I've nothing to live for!

Varvara (*with disgust*) Don't bother baring your soul. You're not the only one who broke the vows of his youth. There are thousands and thousands of traitors.

Ryumin (*shattered*) Then it is farewell. I understand now. I was too late. I took too long . . . But you know, Shalimov isn't any . . . Take a long, hard look at him and –

Varvara Shalimov? What right have you to speak to me of Shalimov?

Ryumin None.

Ryumin exits. Varvara sinks to the ground. Suslov enters, picks up a bottle, drinks from it. Varvara sees him and quickly exits into the woods. Ryumin re-enters, looks around for her, makes a gesture of annoyance, and sits down on the straw.

Suslov (*drunk*) I say, did you hear it?

Ryumin Hear what?

Suslov The argument.

Ryumin About . . .?

Suslov (*lights a cigarette*) It was Vlass, and the writer, and Zamislov.

Ryumin No.

Suslov You didn't? Pity. It was a cracker.

Ryumin Don't set fire to the straw!

Suslov Sod the straw. God it was a cracker! Same old shit, though, if you ask me. I went in for philosophical debate myself, once upon a time. I could spout all the jargon – Hegelian dialectic, bourgeois hegemony, direct action – plus, I knew what it meant. But it's all dead, d'you see? Dead ideas. Man is an animal, and no matter how much bollocks he talks, in the end all he wants is to eat, sleep and shag. Am I speaking an inextinguishable truth? Yes, comrade, I am! When Shalimov opens his mouth, I understand – he's a wordsmith, that's his trade. And when Vlass opens his mouth, I understand – he's young, and profoundly stupid. But when Zamislov opens his mouth – that cheating, grasping swindler – I want to smash my fist in his face! Heard how he's lured Bassov into some shady deal? He has, you know. Totally illegal, and they'll make fifty thousand each. But the name of

Bassov, and the name of that dandified con-man, will be mud for ever after! Hell's bells, they will! As for stuck-up Varvara, who can't make up her mind who to take as a lover –

Ryumin That's enough! You exude filth.

Ryumin exits quickly.

Suslov (*shouts after him*) Ah, you gutless worm!

Pustobaika enters, takes his pipe from his mouth and stares at Suslov.

Suslov What are you looking at? Piss off!

Pustobaika exits slowly. Suslov lies back on the straw.

Ah, they're all villains . . . all of them, behind the mask . . . 'The love of money is the root of all evil.' What a load of cock. Money means nothing. If you've got it. (*getting sleepy*) The opinion of others, though . . . there's something to send shivers down your spine . . .

Suslov falls asleep and snores loudly. Dudakov and Olga enter, walking arm in arm, she gazing into his eyes.

Dudakov We were both in the wrong. We both lost our heads a little, and, ah, so to speak, lost our respect for each other. Fact is, I can't see why you would respect me . . . What am I, after all?

Olga You're the father of my children, Kirill, and I love you, my treasure.

Dudakov I get tired, d'you see, and I, well, I lose control, I suppose. Nervous exhaustion. And Olga, you – you take everything so much to heart. And so we create our own private hell.

Olga But you're all I have in the world! You and our little ones! I've nothing else, nothing.

Dudakov Do you remember, Olga, how we, how way back in the distant past we, well we didn't dream it was going to be like this, did we?

Yulia enters with Zamislov.

Not remotely like this.

Olga But what could we have done? We have children to feed.

Dudakov Yes, the children. I know. But sometimes I wonder if –

Olga Oh, sweetheart! We've done our best.

They kiss tenderly, and exit into the woods.

Yulia (*laughing*) How touching! No doubt I should follow their example.

Zamislov That was the preamble to child number five – or is it six? Well, gorgeous Yulia – will you keep our rendezvous?

Yulia Don't know, do you think I should? Weren't they sweet! Shouldn't I step back on the path of virtue, too?

Zamislov Nothing to stop you doing that afterwards.

Yulia Afterwards, then. Lead me down the path of vice, and let my dacha romance die a natural death.

They kiss.

What caused the fireworks with Vlass and the writer?

Zamislov Vlass is off his head today. We got on to the subject of faith.

Yulia So what do you believe in, then?

Zamislov Me? I believe in myself. Only in myself. My right to live any way I want. And you?

Yulia I don't believe in anything at all.

Zamislov When I was a kid I went hungry. I have a long history of humiliation, Yulia. It was pretty bleak. But I somehow came through it . . . Now I'm the master of my own destiny. And I'll do whatever's necessary to keep it that way. – I have to go. Goodbye, luscious. – You know, we ought to exercise a little caution. Keep a safe distance, in public.

Yulia No distance is safe, my Romeo, from you . . . But what do we fear? Our love is wild!

Zamislov It is, but, nevertheless . . . I think the time has come for me to vanish.

Yulia Like a wood-sprite!

Zamislov Just so.

> *Zamislov exits into the woods, blowing her kisses.*
> *Yulia watches him go and sighs deeply.*

Yulia (*sings*)
The mother rocks her baby
But no-one cradles me . . .

> *She sees Suslov. She stands motionless, looking at him.*
> *With a smile, she sits down next to him, and tickles*
> *his face with a piece of straw. Suslov groans and*
> *wakes.*

Very musical.

Suslov Wha –? What in hell? You.

Yulia You stink of wine. I can't smell the countryside. I can only smell you. You'll drink yourself into the grave.

Suslov (*reaching for her*) You, so close . . . I forget, Yulia . . . When did we last ?

Yulia I wouldn't waste time trying to remember. Listen, do you want to give me pleasure?

Suslov Oh yes, yes! Tell me how! I'll do anything.

Yulia You are such a loving husband, aren't you, Pyotr?

Suslov (*kissing her arm*) Tell me what you want to do.

Yulia takes a small pistol from her pocket.

Yulia I want us to shoot ourselves. First you, then me. Let's!

Suslov What an appalling joke! Throw it away, throw that ghastly thing away! Will you please do so, now?

Yulia Get off! Don't you like my proposition? You said you were going to shoot *me*! I'd be entirely happy to kill myself first, but you'd cheat, wouldn't you? And I won't be cheated any more. And I simply couldn't *bear* to be parted from you . . . I think I shall live with you for ever such a long time. Doesn't that make you glad?

Suslov (*crushed*) I say, you can't treat a man like this. It isn't done.

Yulia You won't play the game? I'll just shoot you, then, shall I? It's a darling little pistol, isn't it?

Suslov I don't give a shit what it is, stop pointing it at me! What the hell is this about? I've got to get away from you.

Yulia (*gaily*) Go ahead. I'll shoot you in the back. Oh, what a shame. There's Maria Lvovna. So I can't.

Maria Lvovna enters, deep in thought.

She's ever such a nice lady. Why don't you fall in love with her? Sensational grey hair . . .

Suslov You're driving me out of my mind. Why do you hate me so?

Yulia How could anyone possibly hate you? Far too much effort.

Suslov Then why do you torment me? I don't understand!

Yulia Maria Lvovna! – You've turned me into a demon, Pyotr. I'm going to be devilish from now on. Run away! Get lost! – Maria, are we going home soon?

Maria What? Oh, I couldn't say. They're scattered all over the place. Have you seen Varvara?

Yulia With that so-called writer, probably. (*to Suslov*) I thought you were going? It's quite all right, we won't miss you.

Suslov skulks off. Yulia puts away the pistol.

Maria You're very hard on him.

Yulia Does him good. I'm told some great thinker gave this advice to men: when you go near a woman, take your whip with you.

Maria That was Nietzsche.

Yulia Really? Crazy, wasn't he? I don't know any great thinkers, crazy or otherwise. But if I was giving advice to women, I'd say: when you go near a man, take a good stout club.

Kaleria enters, and sits on the rug.

Yulia I've also heard of a tribe of savages who have an awfully quaint marriage custom. Before taking his bride, the man beats her round the head with a cudgel. Since we, of course, are civilised, we do it after the wedding. Were you beaten round the head with a cudgel?

Maria I was indeed.

Yulia The savages are less hypocritical, don't you agree? – Why are you sad?

Maria Oh, don't ask . . . Are you unhappy too?

Dvoetochie enters, holding a fishing rod.

Yulia Me? What a suggestion! (*Laughs.*) I'm always sunny.

Dvoetochie Lost my damned hat! It just floated away . . . Some young fools tried to rescue it, and sent it to the bottom. Ah well . . . Has anyone got a scarf I could put on my head? The mosquitoes, see, go for my bald patch.

Yulia Hang on, I'll find something.

Dvoetochie We had a right laugh out of young Vlass a minute ago. He's a card and no mistake!

Maria How was he? Cheerful?

Dvoetochie Happy as a sandboy! Yep, full of beans. Treated us to some of his poetry. There was this little girlie wished him to recite, so he says:

I looked into your eyes
And found to my surprise
That since that blissful peep
I can never get to sleep!

Genius, eh? Then he goes:

Maria (*quickly*) I think I've heard those verses, thank you. Tell me, will you be staying here long?

Dvoetochie Ah, well. I had a mind to see out my days at my nephew's place. But he doesn't seem wildly keen. Got nowhere else to go, though . . . no other relations . . . pots of money, but that's it.

Maria Are you extremely wealthy?

Dvoetochie Couple of million, give or take. (*Laughs.*) All right, three. And when I kick the bucket, Pyotr'll get it. But not even that seems to tempt him. He's not very loving to his old uncle. I suppose he has everything he needs . . . and he'll get the cash anyway . . . so why exert yourself?

Maria (*with great interest*) You know, you could always put that money to use somewhere else . . . something of social value . . . Don't you think that might be more rewarding?

Dvoetochie Hmm. Yes, could be. I met a fellow who gave just the same advice. Only he was French, so I didn't take him seriously. He said he was a liberal – but he had red hair. – Speaking to you very frankly, it does seem a shame to leave it all to Pyotr. What's he going to spend it on? He's got a few too many funny habits as it is.

Maria laughs.

What's so comical? Think I'm stupid? I'm not stupid, oh no. Just don't fancy living alone. Ah, well . . . Once you start feeling sorry for yourself, before you know it you're feeling sorry for everyone else, too! And we can't have that! You're all right, you are.

Yulia approaches, carrying a scarf.

Yulia Are you flirting with Maria, Uncle?

Dvoetochie No such luck. Too old for that now. There was a time . . .

Yulia I'm sure there was. (*She ties the scarf round his head.*)

Dvoetochie Tie it on nice and tight. Then I'll have a little bite to eat.

Yulia Suits you!

Dvoetochie Don't tell fibs, you. I've got a manly face, I have. Come and have a sandwich.

He draws Yulia away.

Dvoetochie Now then. I've been meaning to ask you something. You don't love your husband, do you?

88

Yulia Could anyone love him, in your opinion?

Dvoetochie Why did you marry him, then?

Yulia He pretended he was interesting.

Dvoetochie (*laughs*) Oh well, God bless!

Yulia exits. Bassov – who is drunk – and Shalimov enter. Sonya enters and joins the party by the rug.

Zamislov (*off*) My lords, ladies and gentlemen! It's time to go home!

Bassov First-rate spot, eh, Yakov? Haven't we had a marvellous time?

Shalimov You've spent the day staring down the neck of a bottle. Sitting and brooding.

Sonya is re-tying Dvoetochie's scarf. More laughter. Zamislov enters, picks up a bottle of wine, and approaches Bassov. Bassov flops down on the straw.

Bassov Yes, and now I'm going to sit some more. You can only appreciate nature sitting down. Forests, trees, woods, branches . . . straw . . . oh, I love nature. (*sadly*) Love people too. I love my poor, vast country . . . my ridiculous Russia! I love everything and everybody! I have a soul as tender as a peach! – You can use that, Yakov. Soul as tender as a peach.

Yakov Thanks, I'll make a note.

Sonya Mr Dvoetochie, will you keep still!

Dvoetochie (*breaking away*) No, that's enough! You'll have me looking like an old granny!

They all laugh good-naturedly at him. He joins Bassov.

The next person who laughs, I challenge to a duel!

They laugh some more.

Bassov Ah, more wine! I'll have a drop.

He takes a glass of wine from Zamislov.

Excellent! Aren't we having a smashing time, my friends? Life is a many splendoured thing, if you see what I mean! If you've got the right outlook, that is. You have to make friends with life. You have to trust it. You have to look at it with the eyes of a child, and everything will be . . . excellent!

Dvoetochie laughs at him.

Friends! Let us look with the eyes of a child, deep into each others' hearts! – Uncle Semyon is laughing at me. Uncle caught a trout, a jolly little trout. So I took the jolly little trout and I put it back, into its natural habitat. Why? Because I am a pantheist. And pantheists love everything! Including trout!

Shalimov Sergei, you're a windbag.

Bassov Judge not, Yakov, that ye be not judged. I've heard you when you get going. You are a man of great eloquence, and I am a man of great eloquence! And as for Maria Lvovna – she's a woman of great eloquence, and worthy of respect!

Shalimov She sprays out words like a machine-gun. On the whole I'm no great admirer of women worthy of respect.

Bassov Very true. Women not worthy of respect are usually worth respecting more than the worthy ones. It's a well-known fact.

Dvoetochie I don't know how you can say that, when you're married to such a princess.

Bassov My wife? Varya? Thing is, old boy, she's a puritan. A saint, but a puritan. Being married to her is like living in church. She reads too much, thinks too much, and is always quoting the latest apostle. But let's drink to her health!

Shalimov Any excuse for a toast . . .

They all drink.

As for Maria Lvovna, now . . .

Bassov Did I tell you? She's having an affair with my clerk. It is absolutely the case! I saw him on bended knee, declaring his love!

Dvoetochie I think perhaps . . . better keep that to yourself.

Dvoetochie walks away. Kaleria approaches them.

Bassov Oops! Sorry. State secret.

Kaleria Sergei, where is Varya?

Bassov Ah, it's my sister, my multi-talented sister. Yakov, have you been treated to her poems? God, you ought to hear them! All clouds, and sky, and generally mountains, and more sky, and –

Kaleria You're drunk.

Bassov A wee bit tipsy. Only had the one glass –

Zamislov – from this bottle.

Shalimov I should be interested to cast my eye over your poetical experiments, Kaleria.

Kaleria I might take you at your word, and bring you four fat notebooks.

Shalimov I don't frighten easily.

Kaleria We shall see.

Yulia (*off, singing*) Time to go home . . . Time to go home . . .

Zamislov drifts off in the direction of her voice.
Bassov winks at Shalimov, and whispers something
in his ear. Shalimov laughs. Kaleria goes back to the
main group. Sasha enters and joins them.

Kaleria Is it time now?

Sonya Yes. Everyone's tired.

Kaleria Whenever I go on a journey, I always set out full
of hope . . . And whenever I return, it's gone. Does that
happen to you?

Sonya No.

Kaleria It will.

Sonya You get a lot of enjoyment out of being gloomy,
don't you?

Kaleria Well, you spend hours in the company of filthy,
ragged people. I'm astonished you can bear it. Aren't you
repelled by all that dirt?

Sonya You know, Kaleria, they've made a major scientific
discovery about dirt. Apparently, if you wash it with
soap, it comes off.

Shalimov You possess a vicious tongue, Sergei. Take
care. You've a wife, too.

Shalimov walks away from Bassov. By the rug,
Sasha, Sonya and Pustobaika are gathering up the
picnic things. Varvara enters, holding a bunch of
wild flowers.

Vlass (*off*) Who's coming in the boat?

Bassov Varya . . .? I'm all alone.

Varvara How much have you had to drink?

Bassov Hardly anything.

Varvara You shouldn't drink brandy, it's bad for your heart.

Bassov I was drinking lemonade, mainly. – Don't cross-examine me, Varya! You're too damn strict. And I'm a gentle soul . . . I'm in love with everything, especially trout, and my eyes are the eyes of a child . . . Sit down, my dear. Let's have a serious talk, a tender talk, the time has come . . .

Varvara Don't be idiotic, Sergei. We're all set to leave. Stand up.

Bassov (*struggling*) Not as easy as it looks . . .

Varvara (*helping him*) Now take yourself down to the boat.

Bassov Yes, dear. Which way? This way?

Varvara (*turns him round*) That way.

Bassov That way?

> *Bassov staggers off. Varvara watches him sternly. She sees Shalimov looking at her.*

Shalimov What a long face. Are you tired?

Varvara A little.

Shalimov I am. Tired of looking at these people. And of seeing you amongst them. Am I speaking out of turn?

Varvara I'll tell you if you are.

Shalimov I watch you . . . floating silently through the raucous crowd . . . some cosmic question-mark in your eyes . . . And I too feel the clutch of loneliness.

> *Sonya, Sasha and the others exit to the boat. Varvara offers one of her flowers to Shalimov.*

Varvara Would you like it?

Shalimov A thousand thanks.

Vlass (*off*) Watchman, where's the other pair of oars?

Shalimov It will lie embedded in one of my books. One day, I'll open the book, I'll see the flower, and I'll think of you. Do you find that sentimental?

Varvara (*averting her eyes*) Go on.

Shalimov It must be so miserable for you . . . trapped in a society where they don't know how to live at all . . .

Varvara Teach them to live better!

Shalimov I have no confidence in myself as a teacher. I am an outsider, a passive observer. I don't stand on a soapbox; even if I did, all my art could not inspire these types with courage. Tell me your thoughts.

Varvara Some thoughts are too black to be told. They should be strangled at birth.

Shalimov And make your mind a graveyard? No, you mustn't be afraid of being apart. The air is cleaner on the outside. The picture's clearer.

Varvara I understand you. And I feel as if . . . as if I'd heard someone I knew was incurably ill.

Shalimov (*seems not to have heard her*) You must not doubt my sincerity! Though perhaps you do . . . But let me tell you, when I'm with you I want to be sincere, to be brighter, and better. (*Takes her hand.*) When I'm with you I feel I'm on the threshold of the kind of happiness I've never known . . . It's as if you possess magic powers, that could infuse me with superhuman strength, if only you would –

Varvara Would what?

He glances around. She watches him closely.

94

Shalimov Varvara . . . don't sneer at me, if I . . . do you want me to spell it out?

Varvara No. There's no need.

Shalimov Then you understand?

Varvara I understand. You're not the world's most subtle seducer.

Shalimov No! You don't understand!

Varvara (*simply and sadly*) You've no idea . . . how much I loved you when I first read your books. How I desired you. You seemed so wise, so determined . . . Once you gave a reading at my college. I was seventeen. And from that day forth the image of you glowed in my memory, as brilliant as a star . . . until I met you.

Shalimov Please don't. I apologise. I –

Varvara When I thought I was drowning in pettiness and mediocrity, I'd picture you. You'd give me hope.

Shalimov Try to understand what I –

Varvara And then when finally you came – you were the same as everyone else. What happened to you?

Shalimov Will you let me speak! Why is there one rule for the herd, and another for me? All of you people carry on exactly as you wish, but because a chap's a writer, he must conform to your expectations. Well, why the devil should I?

Varvara Throw away my flower! I gave it to the old Shalimov, the one who was better than the rest of us. Destroy it!

Varvara exits quickly.

Shalimov Jesus! (*He crushes the flower.*) Viper.

Shalimov exits. We hear Zamislov sing in the woods.

95

Zamislov (*off*)
'Night descends, and draws across –'

Yulia (*off, takes up the refrain*)
'– her silken veil of stars . . .'

Dudakov and Olga enter from the woods. Olga is straightening her hair.

Dudakov We're just in time.

Olga Lord, I feel so sleepy!

Vlass (*off*) Get in carefully, you'll turn it over!

Dudakov Shall we go home and, you know . . .?

Olga My dear, sweet Kirill. Let's not forget this day.

Dudakov No. And you won't forget your promise? The, ah, extra, how did we term it, restraint?

Olga I'm so full of joy! Life will be better now, won't it?

They kiss, and exit. By now everyone – except Maria – has gone to the boat. It has got quite dark. Pustobaika enters, picking up litter.

Pustobaika Glory be, look at the mess! That's summer folk, all right. That's all they leave behind: mess. Turn the earth into a garbage dump.

He exits grumpily.

Yulia (*off*) Who's not here yet?

Sonya (*off*) Mama, where are yooooou?

Bassov (*off*) Mama, where are yooooou?

Maria I'm here, Sonya.

Sonya enters at a run.

Sonya We're setting off, Mama! Come on – you'll miss the boat! – What's up?

Maria Nothing. I think I'll walk. Tell them not to wait for me.

Sonya (*calls*) Don't wait for us! We'll walk!

Dvoetochie (*off*) Goodbye!

Sonya Goodbye!

From the boat, we hear the mandolin and guitar.

Bassov (*off*) Let's have some music!

Yulia (*off*) Music on the waters!

Vlass (*off*) Cast off!

Music plays. Laughter. The boat moves away. Pause. it gets quieter.

Maria . . . Why didn't you go with them?

Sonya I wanted to stay with you.

Maria Let's start, then.

Sonya No, sit with me. Please. Sit here. My darling Mama . . . let me give you a hug. There, isn't that better? Now tell me what's wrong.

Maria (*miserably*) Sonya, my baby girl . . . if you knew.

Sonya I do know.

Maria I think not.

Sonya Remember when I was little and I cried because I couldn't do my lessons? Yes? And you would put my head against your chest, like this, and gently rock me . . .

Sonya cradles Maria, and sings softly:

'Lullaby, lullaby, lullaby my baby . . .'

You're the one who can't do her lessons, now. Because if you love him –

Maria Sonya! How do you know?

Sonya Sssh . . . be still . . .

  'Lullaby, lullaby, lullaby my baby . . . '

He's a nice young man. Don't force him away.

Maria My dear daughter! This isn't possible!

Sonya Sssh . . . He's a bit rough and ready, you'll have
to smooth out the edges. You'll teach him to go to work
with love in his heart, as you do, as you taught me to.
He'll be a good friend for me, and we can start a
wonderful new life! – just three of us at first, but then
four, because I'm going to marry that funny old Max. I
love him, Mama.

Maria (*tearfully*) Sonya, my darling, darling child . . .!
You will be happy! You will!

Sonya Max and I will finish our studies, and then we'll
all live together, and work, work to change the world!
We'll be brilliant, the four of us!

Maria . . . There will be three of us, Sonya. You, and
me, and Maxim. And if he is with us, it will be . . . it
will be . . . as our friend. That's all.

Sonya Ssh, Mama. Lie still. There, there. Don't cry.
  'Lullaby, lullaby, lullaby my baby . . .'

*Sonya's voice trembles. Maria weeps quietly. The light
fades.*
    End of Act Three.

Act Four

The set as for Act Two – the clearing in front of the Bassov dacha. Evening.

  Bassov and Suslov are playing chess under the trees. On the terrace, Sasha is setting the table for supper. Inside, Kaleria is playing a sad piece on the piano. An unhurried pace.

Bassov What our country most needs is this: enlightened, benevolent chaps. A benevolent chap is an evolutionist, he's not in a rush.

Suslov Taking your bishop . . .

Bassov Go ahead. A benevolent chap will change the fabric of society gradually, almost imperceptibly – stealthily if need be – but *his* changes will endure.

  Dudakov scuttles on, clutching papers.

Dudakov Wife's not here, is she?

Bassov Not yours, no. Do join us, Doctor.

Dudakov Ah, can't, sorry, in haste – got to get the Medical School report to the printer's.

Bassov Is that really your job?

Dudakov Well, how many people do you think work at the School?

Bassov I don't know, how many?

Dudakov About half of them. Damned, ah, inconvenience, but –

  Dudakov hurries off.

Bassov Ludicrous figure, that Doctor.

Suslov Your move.

Bassov Righty-ho. As I was saying, this is one of the
great lessons I've learnt: we must be benevolent, we must
love our fellow creatures. Misanthropy – fashionable
though it is – is an excess, and should be curbed. When
I first made my appearance in this part of the world,
eighteen years ago, all I had was –

Suslov Check.

Bassov Eh? You crafty . . . How'd you get your knight
there?

Suslov He who philosophises, loses.

Bassov Conclusively proved.

*They concentrate on the game. Vlass and Maria
Lvovna enter from the woods; they don't see the chess
players.*

Maria Believe me, it'll pass, it'll pass. And then – in your
heart – you'll thank me.

Vlass It's too painful, Maria!

*Bassov pricks up his ears. He motions Suslov to keep
silent.*

Maria You must go away as soon as possible. My
darling boy! I promise to write. Work hard, find a good
situation in life . . . Be strong. Never yield to everyday
pressures . . . the trivia and spite. You are a fine man,
and I . . . I love you. Yes. I do.

*Bassov almost chokes with astonishment. Suslov grins
from ear to ear.*

But this is not doing you any good, is it? And it's scaring
the wits out of me. I'm not ashamed to admit, I'm

petrified by the whole business. You'll get over your infatuation, whereas I . . . I would . . . the longer it drags on, the more I'll start to love you. And it would end in disaster.

Vlass No, I swear to you –

Maria It isn't necessary, Vlass.

Vlass Even if I ceased to love you, I would always respect you.

Maria That's not sufficient. Not for a woman who is still in love. There's another thing I must say. I believe it an indulgence to become obsessed with one's private life . . . in these stirring days . . . I would feel guilty. Personal happiness is a side-issue. We have a great fight ahead! You may think me unnatural, but . . . Go, go, my dear! When times are hard, when you need a friend, come to me, I will greet you as my beloved son. Goodbye. (*She holds out her hand to shake his.*)

Vlass Goodbye. I love you so much I think I will weep.

They shake hands.

Maria Remember, fear nothing, submit to nothing. Oh, my God, my God –

They clutch each other in an embrace. They separate.

Goodbye.

Vlass You are my first love. None will ever be purer. Thank you.

Maria quickly exits into the woods. Vlass turns towards the house, sees Bassov and Suslov, and realises they have heard everything. Bassov stands and bows and is about to speak:

Don't you dare. Not a bloody word.

Vlass pushes past him into the house.

101

Bassov Most forceful.

Suslov (*laughs*) Were you scared?

Bassov Didn't know he had it in him! Well aware it was going on, but . . . such passion! Such nobility! Christ, what a pair of comedians . . .

> *Bassov chuckles. Yulia and Zamislov enter along the path from the Suslov dacha. Yulia approaches her husband, as Zamislov slips into the house.*

Suslov All a calculation, though, on her part.

Bassov How so?

Suslov To get him more firmly in her clutches.

Bassov I hadn't thought of that.

Suslov Oh, she's devious, mark my words. Pulled a rotten stunt on me. My old Uncle, on her advice, has given away all his money.

Yulia Pyotr, a man has come to see you.

Bassov Ask us what's just happened!

Suslov Who is he?

Yulia (*to Bassov*) I'm sorry? (*to Suslov*) Some sort of contractor or something. He says it's urgent.

Suslov At this hour? I'll give him a piece of my mind. (*He exits to his house.*)

Bassov You'll never believe what we saw. Here we are, me and your husband, having a quiet game of chess, and all of a sudden there's Maria Lvovna and – (*laughs*) – so it transpires – they're having an affair!

Yulia My husband and Maria Lvovna? (*Laughs.*) How diverting.

Bassov No, no, no, Maria Lvovna and Vlass!

Yulia Oh, everyone knows about that, has done for ages.

Bassov (*covering his surprise*) Yes, but I've got the latest details –

Dvoetochie, carrying parcels, enters with Ryumin.

Dvoetochie God bless you all! Where is the lady of the house? – Look who I found along the way.

Bassov Well hello! The wayfarer returns! (*to Ryumin*) Sun-tanned and handsomer than ever . . . Where've you been, then?

Ryumin To the South. Saw the sea for the first time. Good evening, Yulia.

Yulia You definitely are handsomer, Pavel. I think I'll go and see the sea, too.

Dvoetochie (*to Yulia*) Brought you some expensive chocolates, dear niece, as my parting gift. (*to Bassov*) I'll nip inside, if I may?

Bassov Go on in, my wife will be delighted.

Dvoetochie goes into the house.

Ryumin It really was stupendous there. The sea . . . Music alone, perhaps, can express the grandeur of the sea . . . Standing before it, one feels very small. Man is but a speck of dust, in the face of that eternity.

Ryumin and Yulia go into the house. Bassov packs up the chess set. Varvara enters from the woods.

Bassov Did you know Ryumin is back?

Varvara In the house?

Bassov Yes. And he's replenished his supply of pompous phrases. Varya, you'll never guess what happened! I'm sitting here with Suslov, losing a game of chess, when up pop Vlass and Maria Lvovna – see what I mean? – actually in the process of – *in flagrante*, as it were – a liaison! And you told me they weren't! Well they are!

Varvara Stop it, Sergei. I won't tolerate your vulgarity.

Bassov I haven't been vulgar yet –

Varvara I asked you to keep silent. But you've clearly spoken to all and sundry. Do you have the slightest idea how irresponsible that is?

Bassov God, here we go! Is there any point talking to you at all?

Varvara No. You should think before you open your mouth. And you should consider, when you do, what others might be saying about you.

Bassov About me? They can say what they damn well like about me! I don't pay heed to gossip and rumour. Given my position in the community, I don't need to. And I'm surprised at you, my wife, for intimating that –

Varvara The honour of being your wife is wearing very thin, Sergei.

Bassov Varvara! How can you say that?

Dvoetochie and Vlass come out on to the terrace.

Varvara I say, as you know, what I think.

Bassov Nevertheless, I am entitled to an explanation!

Varvara I'll explain when I feel like it.

Bassov goes grumpily into his dacha. Varvara sits on the terrace steps.

Dvoetochie I've brought you some extremely posh chocolates!

Varvara Why, thank you . . .

Dvoetochie sits on the steps with her, and gives her a package.

Dvoetochie Lashed out on sweets for all the ladies, so you won't forget me. I've never been averse to a bribe. Do you think, in return, I could have a photograph? To keep?

Varvara Of course you can. I'll go and find one. (*She goes into the house.*)

Dvoetochie So, Vlass, we'll be on our way soon, eh . . .?

Vlass The sooner the better.

Dvoetochie Within twenty-four hours. Ah, well. Wish we could persuade your sister to come with us. There's nothing for her here.

Vlass (*bitterly*) Nothing for anyone here . . .

Dvoetochie Very pleased you're joining me, though. It's a pleasant little town. Four days' ride from the next. My house is vast – ten rooms! Stand in one of them and sing a song – none of the other occupants will hear you! Not that there are any other occupants. Just thee and me. You want to hear the way the wind howls through in winter! Holy God!

Sonya enters from the woods.

When you're young, a dose of solitude is a character-forming experience. If you can live with yourself you can live with anyone. But when you get on in years, ah well . . . nice to have some company. (*He sees Sonya.*) Ah, my little mischief! Come and say goodbye! We're on the train tomorrow, and the day after that you'll have forgotten this old goat ever existed . . .

Sonya I won't forget you.

Dvoetochie (*pleased*) No, how could you?

Sonya You've got such a funny name.

Dvoetochie Is that all? Well, I suppose it's better than nothing.

Kaleria comes out on to the terrace.

Sonya Seriously, I won't forget you, I guarantee I won't. You're so good and kind, and so straightforward. I like straightforward people. – You haven't seen my Mama, have you?

Dvoetochie To my disappointment, no.

Vlass She's not inside. Let's go and look for her. She may have gone to the summer-house, down by the river.

Kaleria I'll come with you, if I may.

Sonya, Kaleria and Vlass exit to the woods. Varvara comes out of the house with a photograph, followed by Ryumin.

Varvara Here it is. When do you leave?

Dvoetochie Tomorrow. – That's a charming inscription. Thank you so much. May I say, I've grown to love you, my little flatfish.

Varvara Why would anyone love me?

Dvoetochie Does there have to be, a reason? I don't think that's what it's about. You love a body. That's it. True love's like the sun in the sky – no-one knows what keeps it up there.

Varvara I'm not sure about that . . .

Dvoetochie Why don't you come with me? Your brother is.

Varvara What would I do? I don't know how to do anything!

Dvoetochie Only because you've never learnt. Learning's easy! Vlass and I are going to build a school – no, two. One for boys, one for girls.

Ryumin In order to imbue life with meaning, one needs to accomplish great deeds, deeds which will linger down the centuries. One needs to construct the new temples.

Dvoetochie That's beyond the scope of my ability, that kind of futuristic genius. Left to myself I wouldn't have thought of schools, but a certain kind person enlightened me.

Ryumin Yet even universities offer no more than endless polemic, fruitless speculation and abstraction, mere guesses at the mystery of existence . . .

Varvara (*crossly*) Oh, how trite and predictable . . .

Ryumin looks at them strangely. He laughs quietly.

Ryumin Yes, isn't it? Dead words. Dead as autumn leaves. I speak them out of habit. I don't know why. Perhaps because autumn is advancing . . .? Ever since I saw the sea . . . ever since then I hear incessantly the ponderous thunder of the waves . . . Every word ever spoken is drowned in that symphony, drowned like drops of rain in the depths of the ocean . . .

Varvara You seem ill at ease. Is something the matter?

Kaleria and Vlass enter from the woods.

Ryumin (*laughs*) No, nothing, I assure you.

Kaleria (*to Vlass*) What you call standing on your own two feet means standing knee-deep in dirt.

Vlass You float in the ether, I take it?

Kaleria I've no wish to talk to you. You're rude.

Kaleria goes into the house.

Dvoetochie Given the lady a trouncing?

Vlass sits at Varvara's feet.

Vlass I'm sick of her. 'Oh, I'm dying of *ennui*!' I told her: you live among people, but you die alone.

Ryumin That's true. That's very true. Cruel, but true.

Bassov and Yulia come out on to the terrace.

Varvara (*to herself*) It's as if life takes place somewhere else . . . nothing to do with us. We just contemplate it, from afar.

Bassov Varya, I've asked Sasha to lay up for supper out here. (*to Dvoetochie*) Uncle Semyon, we'll give you a little send-off. We'll open champagne! It's the perfect excuse.

Suslov enters fast from his own dacha.

Dvoetochie Well, I'm touched.

Suslov I say, Yulia, come here a moment.

Yulia What is it?

Suslov takes Yulia aside and whispers to her.

Bassov And for your delectation, my good friends, I shall be serving sausage – and my God, what sausage! Sent to me by a client in the Ukraine. The ideal sausage! – Where's my assistant? (*under his breath*) Or should I say, Yulia's husband's assistant?

Varvara Sergei! That's vile!

Bassov Everyone's aware of it. Don't be so touchy. Sasha!

Bassov goes indoors. Yulia and Suslov return to the terrace.

Yulia (*gloating*) Well, what do you think, Mr Dvoetochie? Pyotr was building a big wall round a prison. And it fell down! (*Laughs.*) Two of the workmen were buried alive!

Suslov (*grinning*) Made her day, that has.

Varvara But that's terrible! Where?

Suslov The other side of town.

Dvoetochie Well, congratulations. You goon! Have you ever set foot on the site?

Suslov Certainly. Nothing wrong with the plans. Contractor's at fault.

Yulia He's never been near the place.

Dvoetochie You should be flogged. Holy God, what kind of men are you? You're too bloody idle, that's what. All of you!

Suslov (*laughs*) I'll shoot myself, shall I? Then you can't call me idle.

Ryumin You won't shoot yourself.

Varvara But Pyotr . . . the men who were buried . . . are they dead?

Suslov Who knows? (*gloomily*) Suppose I'll have to go and see tomorrow.

Olga enters.

Vlass The whole thing stinks.

Suslov You keep your mouth shut, child.

Olga Good evening! It's not so warm now, is it? I'll be needing my fur before long. – Oh, hello, Pavel. When did you get back?

Suslov takes Yulia aside again, and speaks angrily to her. Yulia gives a mocking bow. Suslov exits towards his dacha. Yulia returns to the terrace. Dvoetochie follows Suslov off.

Ryumin This morning.

Olga And come to see us already? You *are* a good friend. Yes, autumn's on the way. So we'll soon be going back to town, where we'll sit behind our thick stone walls, and see even less of each other than we do here . . . more estranged than ever . . .

Vlass (*groans*) Just wind her up and away she goes . . .

Olga But Lord, it's the truth!

Bassov appears at the terrace door.

Bassov Pavel, old boy, would you step inside?

Ryumin goes inside with Bassov, as Kaleria and Shalimov come out. Vlass wanders off towards the trees.

Shalimov (*in a bored tone*) People expect some sort of national renewal to come from democracy, if it ever happens, but what sort of lesser life-form is he, this democrat?

Kaleria How penetratingly accurate. He's barely a vertebrate. His only conscious desire is to fill his belly.

Shalimov And wear shoes on his feet! (*Laughs.*)

Kaleria What does he believe? Does he have a creed?

Vlass (*annoyed*) And what do you believe? Do you have a creed?

Kaleria (*ignoring him*) National renewal will only come from those who hold some higher faith. From the aristocracy of the intellect.

Vlass The aristocracy of the intellect? (*looking around*) Where do you propose we find that?

Kaleria You're not part of this conversation, Vlass! (*to Shalimov*) Let's move over there.

Kaleria and Shalimov go and sit under the fir trees.
They talk in low voices. She is agitated; he seems
weary.

Varvara (*to Vlass*) You are extremely grumpy today.

Vlass I feel wretched, Varya.

Yulia Come down to the river with me, Vlass.

Vlass No, thank you. I don't have the energy.

Yulia Oh but do, please! I have a little something to tell
you.

Vlass (*unwillingly*) All right, let's go. What is it?

Yulia takes Vlass's arm and leads him towards the
woods, whispering to him. Varvara gets up.

Olga (*catching hold of her arm*) Varya! Are you still
angry with me?

Varvara (*thoughtfully*) Angry? No.

Vlass What! The bastard! If he wasn't married to my
sister, I'd –

Yulia Ssh! Ssh!

Yulia and Vlass exit.

Varvara Goodness! What's happened?

Olga Oh, she loves a scandal, the minx. It's no doubt
silly gossip. But I can see you are still angry, Varya.
Lord, it was only words, just words pouring out of me in
an unguarded moment, when I was down in the dumps.

Varvara Let's leave it there. May we? I don't like broken
things that have been mended. And that includes friend-
ships.

Olga Ooh, you're dreadfully unforgiving, aren't you?
Forgive and forget, that's my motto. Couldn't you try?

Varvara No. We forgive too easily. It's a sign of our weakness. And it kills our respect for one another. There's a man whom I have forgiven over and over again. And now I have no value for him.

Olga . . . You're not talking about Sergei, are you?

Varvara looks away.

It's amazing how fast people change. I remember Sergei as a student. A fine young man he was then! No money, of course, but carefree, full of laughter – a brick, his friends used to say. Curiously enough, you've hardly changed a bit. You're just as severe as you ever were. Perpetual frown on your face . . . When the news got out that you were getting married, I remember my Kirill said to me: 'Well, there's Bassov sorted out! He's inclined to be oafish, but with a wife like that . . .'

Varvara Why are you telling me this, Olga? To prove I'm a nobody, too?

Olga What the dickens gives you that idea? Nothing of the kind! It was just memories . . .

Varvara (*clearly, as if passing sentence on herself*) You're right, I am a nobody. I'm powerless, I'm weak. I've known it for a long time.

Sasha comes out on to the terrace.

Sasha The master would like to see you indoors, ma'am.

Varvara goes silently into the house. Sasha follows, as does Olga.

Olga But Varya, you've got it all wrong!

Kaleria (*softly*) Anyone who tells me that truth is knowable is, I think, already dead.

Pause. Shalimov smokes.

Do you find life sad?

Shalimov At times – immensely.

Kaleria Often?

Shalimov It's never exactly fun, is it? I tell you, I've been around too long to be cheerful. And anyway, these are not cheerful times.

Kaleria The life of any thinking person must be counted a tragedy.

Shalimov Yes indeed. Would you answer something frankly?

Kaleria I'll try.

Shalimov Do you like my stories?

Kaleria Oh, hugely! Especially the more recent – they're less locked into reality, there's less of the coarse, less of the flesh! They're subsumed with that gentle melancholia which shrouds the soul, as the clouds cloak the sun at eventide. There are few readers who will have the capacity fully to appreciate them. But these few love you dearly.

Shalimov (*smiling*) A thousand thanks. Did I hear you say you have some new poems?

Kaleria Yes.

Shalimov I should very much like to hear them.

Kaleria (*smiles*) Then you shall.

> *A pause. Shalimov's head droops. Vlass and Yulia enter from the woods. Yulia goes into the house. Vlass sits at a table with his head in his hands.*

Now, if you like.

Shalimov (*jerks upright*) Eh? What?

Kaleria You can hear them now.

Shalimov (*confused*) Can I?

Kaleria (*sadly*) Have you forgotten already?

Shalimov Certainly not!

Kaleria That was quick.

Shalimov We were talking of . . . talking of . . .

Kaleria You asked to hear my poems.

Shalimov Yes!

Kaleria I'll read them now, if you like.

Shalimov That would be divine. It's such a splendid evening . . . yes, read your work, the moment is perfect. I did not forget. I sink sometimes into a reverie . . . the material world dissolves . . .

Kaleria Ah yes . . . (*rising*) I'll fetch them. Though I doubt you really care.

Shalimov Not so, not so, believe me . . .

Kaleria goes quickly indoors. Shalimov pulls a face. He sees Vlass, who is whistling quietly to himself.

Sunk in reverie, Vlass?

Vlass (*pleasantly*) Just whistling.

Dvoetochie and Suslov enter from Suslov's dacha. Both look angry. Bassov comes out on to the terrace and surveys the food which Sasha has laid. He is followed by Olga, Ryumin, Zamislov and Varvara, who leans against a pillar.

Bassov Everybody here? Vlass? Maria Lvovna?

Vlass I'm here.

Yulia comes out of the house and sits on the terrace steps.

Zamislov (*to Varvara*) We are all complex beings, fair lady.

Bassov Yakov too? Excellent, excellent!

Zamislov It's precisely our psychological complexity that makes us the elite of this country, the intelligentsia –

Dvoetochie listens to Zamislov with interest. Suslov goes across to the trees and joins Vlass and Shalimov. Maria Lvovna and Sonya enter from the woods.

Varvara (*angrily*) We're not the intelligentsia! We're just the summer folk. We just pass through. We don't belong here, we don't belong anywhere! We drift about looking for a pleasant place to sit, a nice beauty spot, and we don't do anything except talk!

Bassov As you are proving so conspicuously.

Kaleria enters from the house with a notebook in her hand.

Varvara (*even more angrily*) And we tell such lies to each other! We pollute the air with clever language, to disguise our spiritual desolation! We spout volumes of second-hand knowledge! Life's a tragedy, we say, without having ever experienced it, with no conception of what tragedy is – we just sit about and moan!

Dudakov enters and stands somewhere Olga can't see him.

Ryumin Oh, come on! Fair's fair! If our fears are poetically voiced, they have a certain splendour . . . Never, ever, Varvara, doubt the sincerity of despair . . .

Varvara But why can't we have the courage to keep silent? We're quiet enough when we're content, aren't we? If we find a plateful of happiness, we lap it up alone. But find the tiniest sorrow on the table and we run through the streets gnashing our teeth, crying out 'despair'! In the same way that we poison our towns with sewage, we poison the lives of our neighbours with the effluent seeping from our souls! There must be hundreds, thousands of perfectly healthy people, infected by our whinging and whining! Who gave us the right to spread this disease, to inflict on them our weeping sores?

Pause.

Vlass (*softly*) Bravo.

Dvoetochie Good girl.

Maria takes Varvara's hand. Vlass and Sonya also go to her.

Ryumin (*irritably*) Would you mind if I say a word? My final word?

Kaleria Have the courage to keep silent.

Olga (*to Bassov*) What's got into Varvara?

Bassov Christ knows. Thus spake Balaam's – oops . . .

Bassov covers his mouth with his hand. Varvara has not heard what he said. But the others have understood (Old Testament, Numbers 22 ff). Zamislov walks away, laughing. Shalimov smiles and shakes his head reproachfully. Vlass and Sonya look at Bassov with contempt. An awkward silence. Suslov coughs. Varvara is perplexed.

Varvara Have I said something rude? Why has everyone gone so . . .?

Vlass *You* weren't rude.

Olga (*with a show of innocence*) Lordy, everybody, what is it?

Maria (*to Vlass*) Don't.

Maria starts speaking to cover Bassov's gaffe. She becomes more and more passionate. Shalimov, Suslov and Zamislov make it plain they're not listening. Dudakov nods his head in agreement.

We should try to be different. We really should! We're
the children of cooks and laundry-women and decent
working people. We have a duty to be different! Never
before has our great country had an educated bourgeoisie
with direct blood ties to the working class. Those ties
should feed us, should plant in us a burning desire to
improve and regenerate and illuminate the lives of our
own people – people who toil and toil, till the day they
die, trapped in dirt and darkness . . . We too should
work! Not as an act of charity, but for ourselves, to
nourish ourselves, to broaden our boundaries, and to
annihilate this sense of solitude we feel . . . up here on
our lonely heights . . . looking across the chasm, down
on the poor huddled masses –

*Bassov is grateful to her. He tries to encourage the
others to pay attention.*

Maria – who of course look back at us with sheer hatred,
because we're the enemy, because we live well on the
fruits of their labour! It's as if we've been sent on ahead –
a search party – to find the road to a better life. But we've
lost our way. And we've abandoned them. And we've
created our own bitter isolation, and filled it with anxiety
and little private wars . . . That's our tragedy. But we did
this to ourselves! We deserve our demons! I stand with
my comrade Varya . . . We have no right to moan.

A long pause.

Dudakov Well, ah, there you are. Every word of that is
true.

Olga Oh, that's where you've got to! Come here!

Shalimov My compliments on a fine peroration, Maria
Lvovna. Have you, er, finished?

Maria Yes.

Olga (*leading Dudakov aside*) Did you hear what Sergei said? He made such a fool of himself!

Dudakov What's he to do with it?

Olga Varya was talking such claptrap, he called her Balaam's ass!

Dudakov If anyone's an ass, it's him. Olga, back at, ah, home, there's, well –

Olga No, I'm not leaving! Kaleria's going to recite! Oh, Varya got her come-uppance. She's been so high and mighty of late!

Ryumin, looking crushed, leaves the terrace and paces around.

Shalimov Ladies and gentlemen, Kaleria has very kindly agreed to read her latest poems.

Bassov Dear sister, please do!

Kaleria (*shyly*) If you wish, I'll try . . . Varya? To what do I owe this sudden interest in my poetry? Do you know? I'm now of course terrified.

Varvara My guess is, someone's been offensive, and they're trying to cover it up.

Kaleria Well, I shall read, anyway. I've no doubt my verses will meet the same fate as your words. Swallowed up in the quagmire of our lives . . . (*Reads.*)

On the slow exhale of autumn
Drift immaculate, spent petals –
Immaculate in death –
And crystalline flurries of snow.
And together they embroider
The rank, sullied earth
With a counterpane of pure
White linen.

Dark, dismal birds . . .
Dark, dead trees . . .
Crisp, white snowflakes
Descending from the mute glory of impenetrable skies.

Pause. They all look at her as if expecting more.
Kaleria shuts her notebook.

Shalimov . . . How precise, how exquisite.

Ryumin 'The mute glory of impenetrable skies . . . '

Vlass (*excitedly*) I'm a poet, too. I'd now like to recite some of my verses!

Dvoetochie (*laughs*) Away you go, then!

Shalimov A competition! First rate!

Varvara Vlass – must you?

Zamislov He must, he must, as long as it's witty!

Maria (*to Vlass, softly*) Be true to yourself, remember?

Vlass I shall now demonstrate how absurdly simple it is to stuff people's heads with verse. If I may have your attention . . .?

On the bumpy breeze of autumn
Drift aimless, worthless people –
Immaculate in suits! –
And dithering like headless chickens.
Cheap pleasure is their goal
Or a warm, upholstered hole
To sit and cringe in.

Dark, their thoughts
Dull, their ideas
They spread themselves across the land like dung
Cowards and liars and phantoms with nowhere left
   to hide.

Pause. Everyone is uncomfortable.

Dudakov Fact is, that was well-aimed. Not nice to be the butt, of course, yet . . .

Yulia Bravo, Vlass! I liked it!

Dvoetochie A walloping and no mistake! You're a fighter, you are!

Kaleria Mean and malicious. And why?

Zamislov Not witty at all!

Shalimov Sergei? Your views?

Bassov Mine? Well, God, the rhyme-scheme was pretty weak – only spotted one. But as an amusing little ditty –

Zamislov Rather too close to the bone to be amusing.

Suslov Will you allow me, as a representative of the head-less chickens' faction, to reply to that . . . that hellish . . . it doesn't even have a literary genre! But I shan't address my critique to you, Vlass. Oho no. I shall address the source and fount of your inspiration: Maria Lvovna.

Vlass Watch your step, Suslov!

Maria Me . . .? How bizarre. But I'm flattered.

Suslov It's not bizarre at all, as everyone knows you're the muse of this poet, that your hand holds his – pen – as he writes.

Vlass Don't stoop to innuendo!

Yulia Without innuendo, he's nothing. It's his only tool.

Suslov Don't interrupt, you! – Maria Lvovna, you are, I gather, an idealist. You'd have us believe you're involved in secret plots and programmes, lots of cloak-and-dagger stuff, turning the tide of history et cetera. Well, perhaps you are. Doesn't concern me. But you evidently think that this subversive activity gives you an automatic right to sneer at people.

Maria (*calmly*) Not so.

Suslov You preach at us incessantly. You've taken this tuneless youth and orchestrated him to a pitch of denunciation.

Vlass Stick to words of one syllable, Suslov.

Suslov (*viciously*) You shut your mouth! I've listened to your shit for long enough! – Maria Lvovna, if we don't live our lives in quite the way you would wish, perhaps we have our reasons. Every single one of us here knew poverty in our youth. We all remember what it's like to be hungry. Is it not natural that, in our maturity, we like a good meal and a drink? The chance to take it easy? Aren't we entitled to some recompense, for all the hardship we grew up with?

Shalimov Who exactly is this 'we'?

Suslov Him! Her! Him! All of us! Yes, all of us! We are the children of workers and tradesmen. We went bloody hungry! Did we not? Who will contradict me? It may not be quite to your socialist taste, Maria Lvovna, but we *deserve* our little luxuries, it's natural, it's human nature! Hell's bells, human nature is paramount, and then comes all the other shit! So why don't you leave us in peace? You can criticise us, you can bait others to criticise us, you can call us cowards, hypocrites, but none of us is going to suddenly start doing social work! Not one! Not one of us!

Dudakov You display the most appalling cynicism. It would be altogether better if you'd stop.

Suslov No, to hell with it, I won't stop! And as for me, yes, as for me, let's consider me for a change – I'm no infant. I've grown up. I don't need teachers any longer, thank you, Maria Lvovna. I'm a grown-up Russian man, a common-or-garden Russian man, a philistine if you like. Yes, a provincial Russian philistine, no more nor less! And here is my programme: I shall carry on being a philistine, and I shall do whatever the bloody hell I want! To sum up: I shit on your slogans. And your revolution.

Suslov exits towards his dacha. There is general consternation. Zamislov, Bassov and Shalimov go to one side, talking animatedly. Varvara and Maria go a different way. Yulia, Dvoetochie, Dudakov and Maria form another group. Kaleria stands alone. Ryumin still paces up and down.

Vlass Well, I'll be damned.

Sonya goes to Vlass and speaks to him.

Maria He's having a breakdown. That's the only explanation. You'd have to be mentally ill, to make yourself so vulnerable . . .

Ryumin (*to Maria*) Now do you see how risky the truth is?

Varvara Such pain, such wounded pain!

Yulia Maria, my dear – did he hurt you?

Maria No. He hurt himself.

Dvoetochie (*cheerily*) Holy God, it's like going to the opera, coming here!

Dudakov (*to Olga*) Wait a second. (*to Dvoetochie*) You know what an abscess is?

Dvoetochie Yes.

Dudakov He has an abscess on his, ah, heart. And it burst. Could've happened to you. Assuming you've a heart.

Yulia Nikolai . . .

Zamislov (*going to her*) Did he upset you?

Yulia Not in the slightest. But I'm uncomfortable here. Will you walk with me?

Zamislov Monstrous business. And such a shame, when my boss had laid on a surprise for supper.

Yulia I think I've had enough surprises for tonight.

Yulia and Zamislov exit.

Shalimov (*to Kaleria*) What do you reckon to that?

Kaleria I feel as if all the slime from the bottom of the swamp has risen up and forced itself down my throat . . . choking me . . .

Bassov takes Vlass by the arm.

Vlass What do you want?

Ryumin (*to Varvara*) That cascade of bile has unhinged me . . . broken my spirit. I would have liked to spend a quiet evening with you. A last evening with you. I'm going away for ever.

Varvara You know what I think? I think Suslov's the most genuine of us all. He put it crudely, but he spoke from the heart. How many of us have the guts to do that?

Ryumin (*backing off*) Is that your farewell? Dear Christ . . . (*He exits to the woods.*)

Bassov (*to Vlass*) Well, old boy, let's see, whom have you offended? My sister . . . Yakov . . . highly respected author . . . Suslov . . . and Ryumin. Pretty good going! When would you like to start making your apologies?

Vlass What – me apologise? To them?

Bassov Hey, now, piece of cake, see what I mean? Slip up and say: 'Just poking fun, folks, liven up the party, went a bit too far, humbly abase myself.' You'll be forgiven. They're used to your stunts. Everyone knows you're a clown.

Vlass (*shouts*) You're the clown, Bassov! You're an ape!

Bassov attacks Vlass. Vlass fights back.

Sonya Please, let's be civilised!

Varvara Vlass?

Maria A tidal wave of madness . . .

Dvoetochie (*to Vlass*) Bugger off, quick!

Bassov Thing is, I'm now a little bit piqued.

Varvara Vlass, did you have to –

Bassov An ape?

Vlass It's only from respect for my sister that I don't –

Varvara Vlass! No!

Sasha enters from the house.

Sasha Shall I serve supper?

Varvara Go away!

Sasha (*to Dvoetochie*) I think I'll serve. Food on the table will calm the master down.

Dvoetochie Get out of it!

Bassov (*to Vlass*) I ask you, sir – I, an ape? A man of my standing? And what are you? – A snot-nosed boy.

Kaleria Sergei, be still.

Bassov He's a snot-nosed boy! It's a well-known fact!

Bassov attacks Vlass again. Shalimov takes Bassov's arm and leads him towards the house.

Shalimov I think we can cease hostilities, old chap . . .

Maria Vlass! I'm ashamed.

Vlass What have I done? I'm not to blame!

Sasha Master? Shall I slice the sausage?

Bassov How the devil do I know? I'm a nothing. In my own useless house, I'm a nothing!

Shalimov takes Bassov into the house. Sasha follows.

Maria (*to Sonya*) Take him to our place. (*to Vlass*) Go with her.

Vlass Oh, please, forgive me! Whatever I did, forgive me! Varya, I'm sorry. Oh, God, you poor woman. Get away from here!

Varvara (*quietly*) Where? There's nowhere to go.

Dvoetochie You can come with me.

Nobody hears him. He exits towards Suslov's dacha.

Maria Varya, you go to my house, too.

Varvara I'll come later. Vlass? I'll come later.

Varvara goes into the house. Maria follows her. Vlass and Sonya exit to the woods. Kaleria, looking stunned, goes into the house.

Olga Heavens above, what a scene! And all of a sudden, out of nowhere! Kirill, do you understand?

Dudakov Yes, of course I do. Only a matter of time till we started to claw at each other. And, ah, fact is, the time has come! Vlass hit the bull's-eye. Damn fine shot! But you better go home.

Olga I'm not going home, not when there's such drama! Could be another twist of the plot at any minute.

Dudakov Most unlikely, Olga. Go back. They're shouting and screaming. The nanny's crying. Volka says she clipped his ear. It's mayhem! I've been trying to get through to you that you simply must go home!

Olga No you haven't!

Dudakov Yes I have! We were there, you were wittering on about Bassov, and I –

Olga No you didn't! Oh, Kirill, you're impossible!

Dudakov Look, what are we bickering about? I said 'get home', clearly and distinctly –

Olga You never said 'get home'! We only speak like that to the staff!

Dudakov Olga, I hate to, ah, mention it, but you are a cantankerous old cow . . .

Olga A what? You ought to wash your mouth out with soap! Didn't we swear solemn vows to –

Dudakov You talk like a peasant.

Olga I talk like a peasant? You smell like a peasant. When did you last –

They exit into the woods. A pause; the stage is empty. It grows darker. Bassov and Shalimov come out on to the terrace.

Shalimov Take it in your stride, my friend.

Bassov But you can see how infuriating . . . A mere boy . . .!

Shalimov That stuff is spewed out daily, in the pages of the proletarian press . . . We learn to shrug it off . . . don't we?

They walk towards the trees. Suslov enters.

Suslov Sergei! I had to come back. I must apologise to you, and to you. I lost my rag. Bloody silly. But she's been hammering me for as long as I can remember . . . She and her activist friends – God preserve us. I hate her face, I hate the way she talks like a pamphlet, I –

Bassov Water under the bridge, old boy. Women are delicate beings, but they do sometimes forget it.

Shalimov (*to Suslov*) You may have gone fractionally over the top . . .

Bassov Oh, balls. Who cares? I'll countersign everything he said.

Unseen, Varvara and Maria come out on to the terrace.

Suslov They're all actresses, that's the nub of it, they're all acting, all the time.

Bassov I know, I've been living with one.

Shalimov We bring it on ourselves. Women are an inferior species. We must never allow them to convince us otherwise.

Bassov Yes, but . . . on a graph between us and wild beasts . . . they're slightly closer to us. To break a woman, you need a firm, but careful hand . . . a benevolent despotism, see what I mean?

A shot rings out in the woods. No-one pays any attention.

Suslov Get them pregnant, that's the secret – as often as possible – then they're easily tamed.

Varvara (*softly*) What utter filth.

Maria It's cancerous . . . Varya, you have to get away!

Suslov exits.

Bassov (*noticing Varvara*) Good God, Pyotr, that was uncalled for! I have to say, you've overshot the mark, there!

Varvara (to *Shalimov, shaking with emotion*) You are a . . . a . . .

Shalimov A what . . .?

Maria Come away, Varya! Come now!

Varvara and Maria go inside.

Bassov Oh, God – they heard us.

Shalimov I shall be leaving tomorrow. Now I'm going to bed. It's cold.

Bassov And my sister's bawling. Oh, God!

Bassov and Shalimov go inside. We hear a watchman's whistle, off. It is answered from the other side. Pustobaika and Kropilkin enter from different directions, in overcoats, with their rifles slung over their shoulders.

Pustobaika All right?

Kropilkin All right?

Pustobaika Any vagrants that way?

Kropilkin Ain't seen none.

Pustobaika Right, you check the engineer's, I'll take a turn round the lawyer's, then we'll meet at the kitchen and cadge a glass of tea off Stepanida.

Kropilkin Bit early, ain't we? They ain't abed yet.

Pustobaika You got to go through the motions, my son. That's the point of security, that is. Show of force.

Kropilkin Right.

Pustobaika Off you go, then.

Kropilkin Right. (*Shivers.*) Damp, it is. Feel the damp?

Pustobaika (*shrugs*) All the fucking same to me.

Kropilkin exits towards the Suslov dacha. Pustobaika notices litter.

More mess. They lives like pigs, they do. Come down here, leave their droppings all over the shop. Summer folk . . .

Pustobaika exits into the woods. Kaleria comes out on to the terrace. Her eyes are red. Pause. There is a shrill blast on a whistle from Pustobaika's direction.

(*off*) Who is it? Holy Jesus! Is it you, sir?

Kropilkin runs on, blowing his whistle. Kaleria watches with apprehension. Pustobaika enters supporting Ryumin, who is bleeding from a wound in his chest. Kropilkin hurries to assist him.

Kropilkin He hurt hisself?

Pustobaika Get him to the Bassovs'!

Kaleria Sergei! Sergei!

Ryumin Please, call a doctor!

Kaleria Pavel! It's you! – What's the matter with him? Answer me!

Pustobaika I'm making my rounds and there he is crawling towards me! Bleeding! Says he's wounded!

Bassov runs out of the house.

Kaleria Sergei, fetch Maria Lvovna! Quick!

Bassov What the devil –

Kaleria Quick! He's wounded!

Ryumin Forgive me . . .

Kaleria Who did this?

Pustobaika (*grumpily*) People only shoots themselves round here. Nobody else'd shoot you.

Pustobaika hands over a pistol to Bassov.

Bassov Oh, it's you! Thought it was Zamislov. Thought Pyotr had – Maria Lvovna!

Bassov runs inside. Shalimov comes out, wrapped in a shawl.

Shalimov What's happened?

Kaleria Does it hurt badly?

Ryumin I'm ashamed . . . I'm so ashamed . . .

Shalimov (*peering*) Possibly not too severe.

Ryumin Please, take me away from here . . . I don't want her to see me like . . . I beg you, take me away!

Kaleria (*to Shalimov*) Fetch help, can't you!

Shalimov exits to the Suslov dacha. The sound of running feet – shouts and cries. Maria Lvovna, Varvara, Vlass and Sonya enter. Maria takes command.

Maria Remove his jacket. Carefully! Sonya, help me. – Stay calm, now, you'll be all right.

Varvara Oh, Pavel . . .!

Ryumin Forgive me! I lingered . . . took too long . . . lost my nerve! And when your heart is small and beating so hard . . . it's easy to miss . . .

Varvara But why? Why?

Kaleria (*to Ryumin*) It's cruel, cruel and vicious! (*Stops herself.*) What am I saying? I'm sorry.

*Suslov, Dvoetochie and Shalimov enter from the
Suslov dacha. Zamislov and Yulia enter from the
woods. Dudakov and Olga follow.*

Maria Here's the exit wound . . . it's not too bad . . .

Ryumin Varvara, give me your hand.

Varvara But what is all this about?

Ryumin I love you! I can't live without you!

Vlass (*through gritted teeth*) Damn your love! Look
what it's done!

Kaleria Hush! He may be dying.

Maria Will you all please stand back! (*to Ryumin*) Don't
be afraid . . . it's minor . . . And here's another doctor,
so we should be able to save you. (*to Dudakov*) Bullet's
passed through. Think I've stemmed the bleeding.

Dudakov (*inspecting Ryumin*) Well, let's see . . . Bullet
wound to the, ah, shoulder. What kind of a suicide
shoots himself in the shoulder? Aim for the head next
time – straight in the head – if you're serious.

Maria Kirill, whatever are you saying?

Dudakov Oh, ah, beg your pardon . . . (*to Ryumin*) Keep
your finger on that – Now, carry him into the house.

Bassov Into our house?

Ryumin I think I can walk.

Bassov Our house, Varya?

Dudakov (*to Ryumin*) You can? Splendid.

Ryumin staggers. Bassov and Suslov support him.

Ryumin Well, there we have it. Made a complete hash of
living – and a complete hash of dying, too.

Ryumin, Bassov, Suslov and Dudakov go indoors.

Yulia I'd say that was fairly astute.

Zamislov What a hopeless farce!

Pustobaika (*to Dvoetochie*) It was me and him found him. Saved his life, like.

Dvoetochie Well done, lads.

Pustobaika Customarily we'd hope for a drop of vodka, for saving a man.

Dvoetochie You're a hard-hearted bastard, aren't you?

Dvoetochie gives a few coins to Pustobaika.

Pustobaika (*insincerely*) Very generous of you, sir. (*to Kropilkin*) All right?

Pustobaika and Kropilkin exit.

Kaleria (*to Varvara*) Will he die? I should have done it myself. Shouldn't I, Varya?

Varvara Don't say that! Oh, how repulsive we are!

Shalimov (*to Maria*) Bad wound?

Maria Not really.

Shalimov A morbid affair, though . . . Varvara, may I just –

Varvara (*with a shudder*) What now?

Shalimov Not so long ago you overheard –

Bassov, Suslov and Dudakov enter.

Bassov We've put him to bed.

Varvara (*to Shalimov*) No! I don't wish to hear your explanations! I shan't believe a single word! I hate you from the bottom of my heart, you vile, revolting beasts!

Vlass Wait, sister. I've something to say. (*to the others*) I can see now that you're all in disguise. You're like actors in costume. You clothe yourselves in the trappings of humanity, but you have none. And I shall dedicate myself, from now on, to stripping off your cover, and exposing your lies, your vulgarity, your lack of any decent human feelings!

Shalimov shrugs and withdraws to the side.

Maria Don't go on – pointless.

Varvara No, let them hear it! I've paid dearly for this moment, for the right to tell them what I think. They've poisoned my entire life! Was I born like this, all twisted and maimed? No! I don't have belief, I don't have strength, I have nothing to help me through life! They did this to me. I wasn't always this way . . .

Yulia I think I could say the same.

Olga (*to Dudakov*) Look at Varvara. Look at her face. All screwed up with malice.

Dudakov (*disgusted*) Oh, God

Dudakov brusquely walks away from her, and exits into the woods.

Bassov Varya, that's enough. Ryumin is a fool. But there's no need to bust everything up because of him, if you see what I mean.

Varvara Be quiet.

Bassov My friend . . .

Varvara I'm not your friend, I was never your friend, you were never mine! We were husband and wife. Complete strangers. And I am leaving you.

Bassov Leaving me . . .? To go where? Varya, people are listening!

Varvara People? What people? I don't see –

Maria Come, Varya –

Yulia Let her speak!

Dvoetochie Strewth, this is a sorry day . . . a sorry day . . .

Varvara Yes, I'm leaving, I'm going! As far away as possible! Away from this cess-pit, this decomposing mass, away from idleness and uselessness! I shall find a life . . . I shall find some way . . . to attack you! Yes, I'll attack you! (*She looks around at all of them, and shouts in despair.*) To hell with you all!

Vlass Sister . . .

Vlass takes Varvara's arm and leads her off towards the woods. Maria follows them.

Bassov (*to Shalimov*) Help me, help me! How do I stop her?

Shalimov (*grinning*) The traditional remedy's a glass of cold water, but . . .

Yulia (*to Varvara*) I wish I could come too!

Suslov is watching Yulia intently.

Bassov Varvara . . .! Come back, damn you!

Dvoetochie (*to Bassov*) You've got a lot to learn, you idiot.

Varvara, Vlass, Maria and Dvoetochie exit into the woods. Zamislov exits a different way.

Kaleria (*sobbing*) And what am I to do?

Sonya You can come to us, too.

Sonya takes Kaleria's arm, and they exit after the others. Yulia approaches Suslov.

Yulia (*calmly, ominously*) Well, well, well, Pyotr darling. Shall we go home and continue our life together?

Yulia exits, twirling her skirts. Suslov grits his teeth and follows her.

Bassov What in damnation is going on? Everyone's gone completely weird! Say something, Yakov.

Pause.

Say something! Are you laughing at me? It's serious, see what I mean? All of a sudden – boom! The whole world blows apart! What will I do? What will I do?

Shalimov Take it easy, old chap. An outbreak of mass hysteria . . . Quite common these days, I believe.

Bassov Oh, hell.

Shalimov (*smiling*) Nothing to get an ulcer about. The Suslovs have gone home, to get on with their lives. May I suggest we do the same? Let's open a bottle of wine.

Shalimov takes Bassov by the arm and leads him towards his dacha. Olga stands under the trees, waiting. Dudakov emerges from the woods and walks slowly towards her.

Olga Kirill – is he going to die?

Dudakov (*sighs*) No, no-one's going to die. No-one. Oh, come along.

Dudakov and Olga exit. Shalimov turns to Bassov on the terrace.

Shalimov Don't look for significance in it. There isn't any. It's not important, at all.

Shalimov and Bassov go inside. Pause. Ragged, shadowy figures emerge from the woods: beggars. They slowly surround the Bassov dacha, and stand, with their caps in their hands, begging.
    The End.